POPULAR VOICEWORKS

28 Songs in Jazz, Gospel, R&B, Soul, and Show Styles

compiled and written by
Charles Beale and Steve Milloy

series editor: Peter Hunt

MUSIC DEPARTMENT

OXFORD
UNIVERSITY PRESS

OXFORD

UNIVERSITY PRESS

Great Clarendon Street, Oxford OX2 6DP, England
198 Madison Avenue, New York, NY 10016, USA

Oxford University Press is a department of the University of Oxford.
It furthers the University's aim of excellence in research, scholarship,
and education by publishing worldwide in

Oxford New York
Auckland Cape Town Hong Kong Karachi
Kuala Lumpur Madrid Melbourne Mexico City Nairobi
New Delhi Shanghai Taipei Toronto

With offices in

Argentina Austria Brazil Chile Czech Republic France Greece
Guatemala Hungary Italy Japan Poland Portugal Singapore
South Korea Switzerland Thailand Turkey Ukraine Vietnam

Oxford is a registered trade mark of Oxford University Press
in the UK and in certain other countries

3 5 7 9 10 8 6 4 2

ISBN 978–0–19–343556–8

Music and text origination by
Barnes Music Engraving Ltd., East Sussex
Printed in Great Britain on acid-free paper by
Caligraving Ltd, Thetford, Norfolk.

Preface

The Voiceworks series is designed as a complete guide and support for anyone who encourages or teaches other people to sing well. *Popular Voiceworks* provides the same support for those who conduct or teach others to sing in popular styles, a catch-all term which for us includes rock, pop and dance music, jazz, gospel and soul, along with some theatre styles too.

Life is full of songs—from karaoke to clubbing, local amateur dramatics to TV advertisements—and singers of all ages, but particularly teenagers and those of college/university age, are often drawn to songs in popular styles. Indeed, most choirs and groups sing some 'popular' material, whether it is songs from shows, songs from the popular culture of TV and radio, or contemporary church music. Yet most of those who work with singers, if they were trained in voice at all, were trained in the honourable cause of creating a vocal sound and a delivery appropriate to songs from the Western European classical tradition.

So this book offers help in a number of forms. First, it includes a set of good, singable songs, which demonstrate some of the richness and variety of vocal sound the popular traditions of the last hundred years have to offer. Of course, the fun of popular music is that it is continually changing, so the book makes no claim to be comprehensive. In the end, a good song is a good song in any style. Second, it covers a range of simple rehearsal and teaching strategies that directors and educators will find useful, to make rehearsals more productive and performances more spontaneous and exciting. Third, it gives down-to-earth advice on how to use the voice safely and effectively, in ways that make popular styles enjoyable and accessible to less experienced singers.

Of course, much good practice in choral and solo singing is universal. Our goal is always to enable those who work with singers to sing well—healthily and safely—in any style they like to sing. But this book focuses specifically on how to sing with authenticity in popular styles. It aims to encourage best practice, and to demystify the skills involved to help groups get the most out of the material they are working with, by using their voices well. In doing so, we aim to enable singers everywhere to express themselves better and enjoy themselves more.

About the Authors

Charles Beale

Born in London and now based in New York, Charles Beale began life as a church chorister and has enjoyed a varied career as a jazz educator, pianist, composer–arranger, and choral director. Author of the acclaimed *Jazz Piano from Scratch* (ABRSM Publishing), he taught jazz and improvising to instrumentalists and singers at London's Royal College of Music, and for ten years he was lead jazz consultant to the Associated Board. His playing and arranging work includes credits on albums and singles by pop and dance artists including Whitney Houston and Adeva and he has been a gigging jazz pianist and MD in London for many years. He recently became Music Director of the New York City Gay Men's Chorus, having for five years been Musical Director of the London Gay Men's Chorus.

Steve Milloy

Steve Milloy has spent ten years coaching and directing singers in schools, churches, theatres, and concert stages across the Midwestern US. A former member of the acclaimed *a cappella* octet *Pieces of 8*, he has sung in popular styles in theme parks and on TV and radio, and has composed or arranged pieces for more than a dozen GALA choruses in the US and UK. Steve has worked at the keyboard and/or on the podium with choruses and threatre troupes in St Louis, Indianapolis, and Cincinnati, and recently he returned to singing and acting in productions such as *The Full Monty* and *Caroline, or Change*.

▢ Acknowledgements

Charlie would like to thank Scott Stroman, Pete Churchill, Kathleen McGuire, Jonathon Welch, Simon Sharp, Nikki Iles, and the many other friends and colleagues from a wide range of musical traditions and contexts over the years, from whom he has ruthlessly stolen (and hopefully adapted!) his favourite teaching ideas about choirs and voice. Let's hope we can pass some of that good stuff on down the line!

Steve would like to thank Sandra Baldwin, Anthony Bassett, Jan Parker, Cindy Sohn and Juliet Jackson, Ronna Paden, Ruthe Ponturo, Ken Hauan, Kelly Butler-Smith, Linda Rees, Patrick Coyle, and the countless other friends and teachers who have influenced me on this journey. Last, but not least, I'd like to thank Charlie for saying, 'Ya know, we should take all this stuff we know and make a book out of it!'.

Contents

Introduction

Popular Voiceworks includes songs in a wide range of popular styles, from simple unison melodies to four-part 'showstoppers'. Many of the songs are newly written for this collection, while there is also a selection of new arrangements of well-known favourites. The material is ordered roughly progressively, and there is a range of styles within each section. It is truly impossible to give a representative sample from such a diverse range of popular music and jazz, but there are songs from many of the major periods from the 50s onwards, with backing tracks that add authenticity and simple piano parts. Some songs are more suited to upper or lower voices, while others are flexible enough to accommodate different voice types. The book divides into the following sections:

Section I: Getting Moving. A selection of simpler songs mostly in unison and two parts, with generally narrower pitch ranges and slower speeds. Enjoyable workshops provide a secure technical grounding for less experienced singers.

Section II: Moving On. Songs with more scope for personal input and a slightly greater technical demand at times. The workshops introduce singers to skills and concepts needed to make a more technically advanced and authentic sound in these styles.

Section III: Showstoppers. The songs and arrangements featured here are more spectacular and sometimes more involved—perfect to close a show, add a dance routine, and show off the skills and enthusiasm of your choir or vocal group.

Each song is accompanied by advice on teaching and rehearsing, laid out as follows:

- **Information**. History or brief background to the piece, to put it in context.
- **Starting**. Suggestions for positioning singers and preparing them for the session ahead; activities for getting started physically and vocally to support the learning of the piece.
- **Teaching and rehearsing**. Step-by-step guide showing how to teach the songs and how best to facilitate learning.
- **Ideas**. Extension ideas for taking the music further and developing the confidence and abilities of the singers.
- **Improvising toolbox**. Simple, fun strategies to get beginner improvisers singing.
- **Listen out**. Troubleshooting: a short list of problems that may arise, how to listen out for them, and how to prevent or correct them.
- **Performing**. Suggestions and ideas for performing the songs.

Each song is headed with relevant CD track numbers. There are performances of all the songs and backings for most. As is appropriate for music in these styles, the performances demonstrate the spirit of the music rather than necessarily the letter, as well as some of the ideas in the workshops. The chord symbols are intended to give accompanying instrumentalists the outline of what to play. For simplicity, extensions and other details have often been omitted, except where essential to the musical character.

Teaching, rehearsing, and directing

Teaching from notated parts and by ear

Think about when using stave notation is helpful, and in some cases whether to use it at all in the learning process. Use notated parts at times but create a way of working that implies that singing from memory is a regular and important part of the way your group works.

Advantages of teaching from notated parts:
- Educators often feel more comfortable.
- For singers who can read music, reading can be quicker.
- All singers need the skills of reading stave notation.

Advantages of *not* teaching from notated parts:
- The song is really internalized.
- Non-readers are not excluded.
- Communication in performance is enhanced with no paper barrier between you and the audience.
- A focus on sound, phrasing, and inflection detail can make for greater authenticity, rhythmic energy, and flexibility of form and phrasing.
- Conventionally, notated parts are rarely seen in performance in these styles.

Teaching by ear is an area many teachers are less experienced in. Here are some guidelines to get you started:

- Learn the song yourself first.
- Plan how to teach the overview map. Is there a verse or chorus form? Which section is the easiest and will achieve a feeling of early success? Should you teach melody or words separately at all or simply do it all together?
- Divide phrases up into manageable chunks and pace the learning carefully. If in doubt, learn less material thoroughly and repeat until really internalized, rather than ploughing through more material in less depth.
- Teach the correct notes the first time, with great precision, as this saves messy re-learning later.
- Teach the whole performance from the beginning, and not just the 'notes'. Discuss the emotional character and mood straightaway, and repeat for phrasing, dynamics, and other musical details including pitch and rhythm; nearer the performance, do runs simply for words, especially later verses; discuss the group's mental map of the song by asking questions like, 'What comes after the second repeat of the chorus?', and 'How many times does this section go round?'.

The song as the basis

See the songs in this book as the *basis* for the performance, and not the performance itself. The arrangements are often adaptable to suit the needs and creative ideas of the group or soloist. Here are the sorts of questions you might want to decide as leader and negotiate with your group:

- **Key**. Would a higher or lower key suit your group better?
- **Form**. What order should the various sections be sung in to best create the mood you want? How many times should repeated sections go round?
- **Backings and harmonies**. Use the ones given to start with, but would others suit your singers better? Do they have their own ideas?
- **Group, sub-group, or soloist**. Should the song be sung by the whole group throughout? Could a soloist or subsection within your group do a good job in a particular section? How can you create variety within the song? Are there any particular personal or musically intimate moments?

When to take the lead

What should your role be in rehearsal? Conductor/director? Facilitator? Should this role change in performance? What conventionally happens in music of this style? Here are some possibilities:

- Direct from the front.
- Direct while singing within the group.
- Pass the direction to a member of the group.
- Allow the rhythm section (piano, bass drum) to keep the time going, while you direct the form and dynamics only.
- Lead yourself from the band or side, on tambourine or piano.
- Have no leader at all in performance. Allow the group to run itself, so they internalize the expression.

A system of hand signals can be useful to facilitate some flexibility in performance. Try:

- *Verse*: both hands in a 'V' shape
- *Chorus*: make a 'C' shape with thumb and first finger
- *Round and round*: first finger circles in the air
- *Go on this time*: first finger points forward
- *Add backings*: tap your back or first finger points backwards
- *Unison*: flat horizontal hand, palm down
- *In harmony*: hand vertical, palm towards your chest, fingers spread

Add your own signals as necessary. Make signals big in rehearsal and scale down in performance as necessary. These can also be done from the drums or keyboard. Anticipate the need for signals and, if there is time, give the group eye contact before each one, to ensure all are watching.

Keeping it loose

Many popular songs—especially in jazz, soul, and gospel styles—are flexible, at the level of both form (how many times things go round, solo sections, the order) and phrasing. Don't be afraid to adapt and add to pitch and rhythm elements, to enhance and personalize the material and fit it to the context. These adaptations might include:

- Modifying the form to suit the length and mood required.
- Changing the key to suit your group or soloists, and perhaps adding a key shift up a semitone on a repetition to create or release tension.
- Practising solo sections.
- Adding written or invented backings and harmony parts.
- Adding new sections for solo or group improvising by instrumentalists or singers.
- Embellishing the given part by modifying the rhythm, pitch, timbre, or vowel sound, or by adding an embellishment, like a fall-off or accent.

If this is unfamiliar territory, all the songs will work in their original forms and examples are given in the text accompanying each song.

As you and your group get more comfortable with the material, explore this flexibility as much as you want to. Don't be afraid to take some risks (initially in rehearsal and later in performance!), as some of the most personal, moving, and exhilarating music can be achieved in the moment, through improvising. If you or your singers are unsure what to do, some improvising activities—simple rhythms, words, and pitch shapes—are provided where appropriate in the 'Improvising toolbox' sections; suggested forms in the 'Performance' sections show you other possibilities too.

Preparing to Sing

◻ Using the voice well and warming up

For singers at all levels, it is advisable to take between 1/4 and 1/5 of the session for warming up and skills development. While other musicians have an instrument, singers have only their bodies to make the sound. A really effective warm up makes the body ready, engages and focuses the mind, and creates the kind of mood where a productive musical experience will occur. From the very beginning, a thorough warm up helps make singers aware of what their voices can do, prevents strain of various kinds, and enables that ideal relaxed, flexible, alert readiness in rehearsal and performance, which actually saves time in the long run.

You can divide most warm ups into the following areas:

Body   Posture   Breathing   Sound   Range   Diction

Whether you have ten minutes or half an hour to warm up, the logic of this order makes it worth covering as follows:

- **Body**. Relaxing and stretching can provide a gentle start. It develops awareness of the whole body, releases tension from previous activities (driving to the rehearsal, science class), and develops good circulation.
- **Posture**. This leads naturally into the process of aligning the body in an easy, natural way that will enable good breathing and a resonant, flexible sound.
- **Breathing**. Once the body is ready, work on the breathing (inhaling, exhaling, and support) which will provide a solid foundation for the voice.
- **Sound**. Once the breath is in place, begin to focus on making an open and resonant sound.
- **Range**. Once you have a sound, explore using it over the widest possible range of pitch.
- **Diction**. Now pitch is more confident, work on accurate and precise articulation and clear communication.

In popular styles of music, it is also good to cover the following areas of skill:

- **Pulse and rhythm**. Much of the music in these styles is based on a groove of some kind. Having some knowledge of a song's rhythmic language helps you to place vocal sounds accurately and idiomatically on the beat, and to use the right sounds themselves. Doing some of the groove-based exercises in this section and in the advice with each song will help make the pulse and rhythm of the song more vivid, the groove more solid, and the sound more authentic. Pulse and rhythm is of course vital in all kinds of music, so work done here pays dividends in every style.
- **Improvising**. Many singers in popular styles personalize the material they sing, and this is a useful and in some cases vital skill, as well as being great fun. In most warm ups, aim to do at least one short exercise which involves individuals or the group making something up for themselves—perhaps some short phrases over a groove, or just choosing some pitches. A group that practises this regularly will quickly become confident at coming up with ideas, and this creates confident singing generally. Embellishing the songs appropriately in a tasteful but authentic way is part of the style.

Finally, include in your warm up ways of warming up the mind as well as the body. This gets the group 'into the right space' to work well together and bonds them through interacting and sharing in a joint task of some kind:

- **Focus**. It can be useful to do a couple of short exercises for developing general concentration and group focus so that the group are all 'on the same page' and ready to work productively and therefore enjoyably.
- **Energy**. Any warm up should produce energy but there can be times, perhaps on a particularly wet day or after a tiring previous activity, when a warm up directed purely towards creating a 'buzz' can be fun and transform the mood.

What follows are simply example warm ups in each of these areas, which cover the main skills and which we have both found work well with a range of musical groups and situations. Further warm-up activites are introduced with the songs, which you can of course adapt to suit your group. Vary your warm ups as much as you can, to achieve some surprises and prevent staleness. At the same time, repeat some key exercises over a number of weeks, as this will create a familiarity and give the singers a sense of progression as they feel themselves improve.

The general warm ups that follow here are particularly suitable for the songs in Section I and cover good practice in general. The warm ups at the start of Section II build on this foundation and also introduce common techniques for singing in jazz and popular styles.

Body

It can be good to play some music through all of these—whether energizing and upbeat, or more relaxed and easy.

- **DIY acupressure**. Make a fist with one hand, like a little hammer, and stimulate the skin by gently tapping on the other arm all over—all the way up to the shoulder and down to the hand, on the top and bottom. Swap, and do the same with the other fist on the other arm. Now use both fists to tap your body lightly all over. Begin with the chest and tummy area and then work down both legs, front and back, and up on to the neck and head. Take a couple of minutes, be thorough, and work in silence. When you have finished, stand still and feel how stimulated your body has become—slightly tingly and very alive. Do you feel more mentally alert too?
- **Big face, little face**. Make a big cheesy grin that involves the whole face and stretches it wide—call that 'big face'. Then scrunch up your face into the middle, trying to make it as 'small' and wrinkled up as possible—call that 'little face'. When you or a group member shouts 'big face!' or 'little face!', everyone should stretch their face into the different positions on demand. Try again with a wider range of faces, perhaps named after emotions found in songs.

Posture

- **Head and neck**. Without straining, begin with the head facing straight ahead. Turn it to the left and hold, then back to the middle. Then turn to the right and hold, then back to the middle. Look up by moving the whole head and hold, then to the middle. Then down, and back to the middle. Close your eyes, and repeat. This time, be aware of your head and establish by feeling rather than looking exactly where your 'middle' is. Check for chins too far up or down. Finish by visualizing your head as very light, floating above your shoulders as if it is carrying the body, supported by a string.
- **Shoulders**. Shrug your shoulders. Lift them high and hold them there in a stretch for around five seconds. Then drop them into their relaxed position, so they hang naturally.

Repeat. Try two dropped positions—drop and then drop again even further. Make sure arms are floppy and loose in the dropped position, like a rag doll. Shoulders should fall not too far forward (rounded) or back but hang naturally in their groove. Explore them being too far forward, then too far back, then in their natural position.

- **Chest**. Reach up as high as you can with both arms. Then imagine a bar above your head, just out of reach. On tiptoe, stretch up, grab the imaginary bar and hold on. Release the arms and tiptoes but stay 'up', maintaining that feeling of relaxed tallness with the rib-cage raised so there is a space below for the breath to fall into. Next, slump forward, so your rib-cage is lowered. In that position, breathe in and feel how little space there is for air. Then stay relaxed but stand up straighter, floating up rather than tensing up. Breathe in again and feel how the lifted rib-cage allows space for breath to fall in. Repeat sitting down, where the tendency is always to sing in a more slumped position.

- **Feel broad and grounded**. Stand with feet shoulder-width apart. Explore your own weight and centre of gravity. With eyes shut, lean forward so you transfer your weight slightly too far on to the balls of your feet, then slightly too far back on to the heels. Do the same, side to side. Then find the optimum balanced position where the weight is divided equally between both. Bounce up and down so you unlock your knees and feel your weight going down into the floor. Imagine your legs as screwed into the floor now, as if you were part of the floor, growing from it like a tree with roots, and supported by it. Feel broad and grounded.

- **Lower back**. Begin by stretching up, feet slightly further apart than shoulder-width. Keeping your feet in position, fall gently forward so that your head and arms are swaying lose. Touch the ground with your hands if you can and bend your knees if you need to. Stay down there a while. Take some deep breaths and, as you breathe out, release in your lower back, so you drop forward that little bit more. Allow a silence. Once relaxed and calm, slowly begin to unroll back up, beginning with the bottom of your back and continuing up, so that your head is the last part to unroll. Continue up to a final stretch with both arms, which should feel as though they are floating up to the ceiling. Then lower your arms but retain the feeling of lightness and buoyancy. Feel the release of tension in your legs and lower back.

- **Hips**. Stand with hands on hips. Sway hips to the left and hold, and then to the right, perhaps in time to some music. Then do the same, swaying the hips forward as far as they will go and then back. Now establish the middle position for your hips and then move them slightly forward, about a third of the way into the forward position, so the pelvis is pushed under very slightly. Take a deep breath and feel the extra support and groundedness that this position gives you.

- **Silly wiggle to finish**. Finish with humour and energy. In this silly question and answer game, wiggle the relevant part of the body in turn as you chant. The aim is to end up upright, relaxed, and loose, with no locked joints. Begin by chanting, 'Oh, I never lock my knees', in a silly voice (high or low, favourite accent), to which the rest of the group must reply in an identical silly voice, 'No, we never lock our knees'. Now continue in an improvised way around the rest of the body, something like:

> You: 'Oh, I never lock my knees'
> Group: 'No, we never lock our knees'
> You: 'And I never lock my ankles'
> Group: 'No, we never lock our ankles'
> You: 'And I never lock my elbows'
> Group: 'No, we never lock our elbows'
> You: 'And I never lock my shoulders'
> Group: 'No, we never lock our shoulders'
> etc.

Next time, perhaps get a member of the group to lead and add a piano vamp on one chord in a style of your choice. If the mood is right, finish by doing the twist or some other dance to imagined music of your choice.

Breathing

Depending on how much time you have, it can be useful to divide this into two sections: 'inhale/exhale' and 'support'.

- **Inhale/exhale**. Breathe normally. Inhale then exhale very lightly, as if at rest. Become aware of the muscles you use to do this. Then repeat breathing deeper, but use only the same muscles. Keep shoulders relaxed, with the chest allowing space below. Your diaphragm and the muscles below it in your pelvic floor are the basis of your air—the diaphragm is the dome-shaped area of muscle that separates your lungs from your abdomen and creates increased volume of air. Find it by reaching up with both hands into a stretch and then leaning gently back, while breathing in. Hold, then lean forward slightly and breath out. Feel the diaphragm move and identify the space where the air falls in. The muscles you use are lower down, and can even include your hips and legs. This is what we call your 'support', and actually involves many muscles throughout the body.

  Breathe more deeply using your diaphragm, in and out through the mouth—some say, as if breathing in and out through the belly button. Try breathing in with an open throat, as if in a slight yawn, so that the air enters silently and makes no gasping sound. Hands by your sides, feel you are expanding out at the sides and from the back as well as the front. Breathe in for a count of 4, hold for 4, breathe out for 4, and relax for 4, keeping the throat open throughout. Try to get really full of air and really empty. Repeat for 6, 8, and, if ambitious, 12 counts. Now breathe out. Hold the air out for 5–10 seconds and, on cue, feel the air fall in.
- **Support**. One function of your support is to create a steady air pressure on which to base a steady, consistent sound. Imagine a candle in front of your mouth and blow it out very gently, using a steady flow of air. Blow it out more firmly, and feel the muscle action lower down in your back, sides, front, and pelvic floor. Next, try going 'mmmm', rising and falling in pitch, as if smelling something wonderful. Repeat, but this time gain more resonance and projection by adding pressure as if blowing the candle out. Now go 'ssssss' or 'vvvvvv' and do the same. For moments of emphasis, try pushing harder, so go 'SSSsssSSSsssSSS' rhythmically on cue. Finally, try very gently making a very short 'ha' on cue. Use no effort, as if a drop of water is hitting your diaphragm and spreading out. Now try two gentle ones—'ha-ha'. Finally, laugh, and feel your diaphragm kicking in.

Sound

- **Loose lips, relaxed jaw**. Make your lips very loose and floppy and do a lip-roll to a 'p' sound, like a horse. Repeat to a rolled 'r'. Go 'yayayayayayaya' or 'mamamamama', ensuring the jaw is loose. Now make a hummed 'mm', keeping lips relaxed so they buzz. Keep the jaw relaxed and feel the space inside, to create resonance and relaxation. Loosen your tongue, licking all around your teeth, top and bottom. Stick your tongue out as far as it will go, and wiggle it around.
- **'mm', 'ng', 'ah'**. Begin by humming your 'mm' on any pitch. As before, drop the jaw slightly and ensure lips are relaxed and floppy, so the whole head 'rings' and the lips begin to 'buzz'. Ask for the sound to become resonant and forward. Allow time for each person to experiment with the exact position of lips, jaw, and tongue. Next, ask everyone to say the word 'sing', and hold the 'ng' sound. Ensure the mouth is slightly open. Some people describe the feeling as though the sound is being 'placed up and forward into the facial mask'. Others describe a laser beam coming out of the top of the head or the space

between nose and mouth. Ensure the breathing remains relaxed and the sound is full but never forced. Finally, gradually turn the 'ng' into a big, open, steady 'ah'. To add further brightness, raise the top lips to expose the front teeth slightly—it looks daft but works wonders. Now ask them to make an inner smile as they say 'ah', raising cheek-bones slightly. Sing the word 'miaow' to keep this sense of a forward sound.

- **Space at the back**. Make a big yawn, and feel the space created at the back of the throat. Say 'ah' through a yawn, sliding from high to low and dropping the tongue slightly at the back. Imagine the space as huge, like a cave or a resonant hall at the back of the mouth. Now sing 'ah' on any note. Add this space into the 'mm, ng, ah' exercise (when you switch to 'ah'). Aim for a sound that is bright but also rounded.

- **The puppy dog whines, the sea-gull caws**. Make a speech-level sound, like a puppy whining (or adult dog if that's too high!), with your mouth and eyes closed. Pay attention to the feeling in your nose, cheeks, throat, and vocal chords. Keeping that sound, slide slowly but smoothly down to the lowest point of your range and hold, paying attention to the sensations from your nose to your chest area. Aim for a feeling of connection with the voice. Slide back up in the same fashion. Start again, but this time, before sliding, gradually switch to a short, repetitive 'caw', like a sea-gull. Maintain the vocal quality and connection you felt before with the 'whine'. As before, slide to the bottom and back to the top of your range, keeping tabs on what's going on in your body.

- **Breathy to focused**. Whisper an 'ah' to start, with no sound. Notice how this dries the vocal cords and make clear that this is to be avoided for long periods. Begin to 'ah' again, but this time add in a small amount of sound, to create a very breathy tone. Note that you are using a lot of air and should run out of breath quite quickly. Starting from there, gradually focus the tone until you find a highly efficient, slightly harsh but very focused tone, which should use hardly any air at all. Ensure you don't push with the air. Then start focused and return to breathy in one long note. Sing a phrase of your choice using a range of breathy and focused sounds. Breathy can sound personal and intimate, particularly with a microphone, while focused is somehow more public and declamatory.

Range

- **Lip-rolls and rolled 'rr's**. Make a lip-roll ('brrr') again and make a speech-level sound with your lips while rolling, sliding the pitch up to the top of your range, falsetto and all, then back down to the very bottom and finally back to the middle. This is a good way to explore your range without straining.

- **Up and down, narrow range**. To explore the top of the range, begin lower down and work up in easy stages. On 'uh' or 'ah', begin by singing one low- to mid-range note, then three notes, e.g.

and then finally five notes. Repeat up a semitone, then up a semitone, and so on, as follows:

Vary vowels as you go, though the most open ones—'ee' and 'oo'—are more complex and work less well higher up, If tense, add *clap* 'whee' after each scale ('whee' is the sound you make when sliding down stairs: a high-pitched falsetto that glissandos down). The 'whee' will relax the vocal chords and prevent tension as you go up. The clap serves to keep the rhythm going and the body moving rather than motionless. As you get higher, tell singers to push themselves with bigger breaths towards the top, but stop before they strain. Also focus on the space at the back of the throat (yawn) to prevent a harsh, nasal sound, and check chins do not stick out towards the top.

To explore the bottom of the range, simply go down from 5–1 of a major scale, as follows:

Aim to take the bright, clear sound you make higher in your register down into the lower notes. Ensure you stay rhythmic throughout, and as you get towards the bottom check that the chin stays in position and does not droop.

- **Leaping up smoothly**. Begin by practising support (blow out candle, etc.), as above. Then sing this phrase, starting low:

Aim for the octave leap to be like a fast glissando, to what is actually the syllable 'ah' with a brief 'ee' at the end. Manage the support through the leap so that the top note is energized but the whole phrase remains balanced. For some singers, the top note may become forced and harsh or stick out. For others, the lower one will lack resonance and need more 'inner smile'. Ensure comfortable breathing, smooth pitch change, and an even tone across the range as you proceed up in semitones. If necessary, make a big movement opening up the chest by circling the arms in a big arc above the head and down as the voice leaps up.

- **Range extension**. The following exercises, sung on a lip-roll or tongue trill (continuous rolled 'r'), are great for creating ease in singing throughout the highs and lows in your voice.

Diction

- **Tongue-twisters and own-choice phrases to scales**. The aim here is to explore the sounds involved, and practise the different movements of the tongue, lips, and jaw, to get clarity without disrupting the line. For example, sing the following, then try it starting with 'co-', 'to-', 'o-', 'e-', and 'a-':

You can also ask group members to suggest words or phrases to sing your scales to—avoid going too high on these exercises. Some examples: football teams, types of pasta, the states of the USA, etc. Different styles of singing demand different kinds of consonants. Sometimes strong, definite consonants can be dramatic and clear, while at other times something smoother and more like normal speech can be less intrusive to the musical effect. For reference, here are the most common single vowels, including some common diphthongs: 'a' (at), 'ah' (father), 'aw' (awful), 'ay' (hate), 'ee' (easy), 'eh' (every), 'eye' (eye), 'ih' (it), 'oh' (know), 'oo' (moon), 'uh' (up). Likewise, consonants: short/long; long voiced: L, M, N, NG, R, TH, V, W, Z; long unvoiced: F, H, S, TH; short voiced: B, D, G, J, K; short unvoiced: K, CH, P, Q, T, X.

Pulse and rhythm

- **Placement**. First, say '1, 2, 3, 4' quietly, round and round, making a four-beat repeating bar. Then clap only on the '1' while whispering, and later omitting, the other beats. When this is in place, repeat, clapping only the '2', then only the '3', and then only the '4'. Repeat, saying the syllable 'bup' (or other single syllable word or sound), or singing it to the groove below:

Once this is in place, another week, do the same with '1–an–2–an–3–an–4–an', saying it first round and round—you are adding the offbeats as 'an'. Then try clapping each of the offbeats ('an').

- **Shoulderin' the beat**. Find a space and, to the same groove, sway your arms back and forth on every crotchet/quarter-note beat—one to the front and one to the back—as if marching. Don't bring them too high and keep them close to your body. Let the elbows relax and bounce. With each sway, bounce your shoulders up and down from their sockets. Add a finger snap on beats 2 and 4. Let the music lead you. Finally, add a vocal sound ('an', 'ha', or 'ho' work well) on the 'and' of each beat. Add voices gradually until you all feel the time together. Let the 'and's gradually find their place in the rhythm you're creating with your body. Aim for a relaxed, even pulse, free from physical tension or rushing.

- **Vocal drum-kit**. Divide into three groups. The first is bass drum ('boom'); the second is snare drum ('chack'); and the third is hi-hat ('ts'). Practise your sounds, then try these rhythms (the second repeating rhythm is harder than the first):

Improvising

- **Choosing single long notes**. Explain that improvising is about choosing and that the simplest choice you can make is one single note. Get a flow going by asking each person to sing a single note, all together, making a big random chord. Explain that whatever comes out is fine—anything at all, no discussion—and go around several times. Then try a longer improvisation, where each group member must breathe in well, sing one note at a time, and then pause for a period. Any pitch may be chosen. Another time, allow them to sing anything from one to four notes, creating the possibility of musical phrases. If time, run a brief hands-up discussion. Discuss beginning to sing. How did it feel? Were you scared to start with, and if so, what were you scared of? If not, help others by explaining why you felt confident. Was it easier second or third time around? Also, ask if they got a sense of a natural place to stop. How long is long enough? Who stopped too soon? Who went on too long? Why? Have another try, and become more aware of the group decision to stop.
- **Riffing**. Begin by teaching the following riff. If possible, play the piano part too:

Then divide into groups of three or four, and give one group that riff to sing. Ask each of the other groups to make up their own riff to go along with the given one. Once one person in the group has an idea, they should teach it to the others. Then begin the first group singing the given riff. Once the initial riffs have been used up, ask each group to make up their own from scratch, with no initial given part. If there's time, harmonize each riff within the group.

Focus

- **'My bonny lies over the ocean'**. Briefly check you can all sing this song, verse and chorus:

  Verse
  My bonny lies over the ocean, My bonny lies over the sea; My bonny lies over the ocean, Oh bring back my bonny to me.
  Chorus
  Bring back, bring back, oh bring back my bonny to me, to me. Bring back, bring back, oh bring back my bonny to me.

Now sing it again, but this time stand up on words starting with a 'b'. Once standing up, sit down on the next one.

- **'1 121'**. Sing a scale to numbers 1–8. Then sing the numbers in unison to this pattern, up to 8 then down again, ending on 12321, 121, 1:

etc., up to 8, then down again

1 1 2 1 1 2 3 2 1 1 2 3 4 3 2 1 1 2 3 4

Once this is OK in unison, split the group in two and repeat in canon, the second group coming in after a minim:

1 1 2 1 1 2 3 2 1 1 2 3 4 3 2 1 1 2 3 4   *etc.*

1 1 2 1 1 2 3 2 1 1 2 3 4 3 2 1   *etc.*

Repeat in up to four parts and, if ambitious, try with each member of the group individually, pointing to bring each of them in.

Energy

- **Magic hammers**. Each person should imagine they have two 'magic hammers', one in each hand, and make the shape of a fist, feeling the weight of the hammer. Then they imagine four sets of nails in front of them: one at head height, one at chest height, one at hip height, and one at their feet. The aim is to bang in the nails using the magic hammers as fast as possible. You or the group choose the number of times it will take to hammer in the initial set of nails—e.g. five movements. To perform the set, you have to hammer in the nails at said level as fast as possible, counting each movement out loud as you do so. Briefly practise the sequence. If the first set of nails takes five bangs, then the whole group will count out loud and 'hammer' in unison, very fast, 12345 four times, starting at head height, then at chest, hip, and finally feet. This will involve moving from standing to crouching position in each round! Next, the whole group goes back to the top, but this time counts and 'hammers' for four nails: 1234 (head), 1234 (chest), 1234 (hip), 1234 (feet). Continue with three nails, then two, then one. Finally, cue the whole activity. Perhaps follow it with a good stretch or shake-out.
- **Big jump**. Stand close together in a circle, all facing the middle. Practise three elements. First, crouch right down. Second, jump in the air as high as possible, throwing arms out in all directions—relax as you land. Third, create a steady group sound to 'oo' or 'oh'—random, low, very quiet, but intense. This is the basis. Next, explain that the 'oo'/'oh' should begin to grow, getting louder and higher. As it does so, the whole group should gradually stand up in their own time. The group sound stays constant—breathe where you want. The group will feel a build-up of energy. They should resist this initially and continue a very slow gradual crescendo. At the climax, after anything up to a couple of minutes, the whole group should release the energy by voicing 'OH!' as loud as possible and jumping as high as possible into the air, as if on springs. Remind the group to maintain the connection between their voice and their support and never shout. All crouch down. Silence. Begin with a quiet 'oo' or 'oh' on cue and let the feeling gradually build. End with that big release of sound and physical energy. This will only work once but is ideal for just before a big performance!

Section I

Getting Moving

1 Swing Time!

RESOURCES ▶ CD1 track 1 (performance); CD2 track 6 (backing)

▨ Information

A five-part round in 12-bar-blues form, this simple song introduces some of the basic elements in jazz/pop music: downbeats and offbeats; syncopation; long and short notes; and the notes of the blues scale. It also makes a great warm up. The popular music of the past century often emphasizes beats 2 and 4 rather than 1 and 3. This evokes a lift in the feel of the music, and a lift in the way you feel towards the music, so the song incorporates this awareness in the first two repetitions. To create that feeling of 'lift' and rhythmic energy in the music, it is good for singers to move.

▨ Starting

- Establish a pulse with some physical movement, tapping your foot or walking on beats 1 and 3, and adding clicks, slaps, or claps on beats 2 and 4. Bend the knees slightly on the offbeats and relax the arms, letting them swing naturally.
- In swing quavers/eighth-notes, say 'du-**vah**-du-**vah**-du-**vah**-du-**vah**', adding weight to the offbeat quaver/eighth-note ('**vah**'). Keep the flow smooth and the tempo steady to establish a groove.
- Introduce the 12-bar-blues pattern by playing bars 3–14 while your singers sing the tonic note of each chord on beat 1 of each bar, like this: 'one, one, one, one, four, four, one, one, five, four, one, one'.

▨ Teaching and rehearsing

- Start with Part 1, which is based on the exercise above. Teach this to the group call and response style, four bars at a time: you sing it to them, they sing it back by ear. Mention that this part stresses the downbeats in each bar. Then do the same with Part 2, which establishes the offbeats (2 and 4).
- While clicking, slapping, or clapping on beats 2 and 4, use call and response to teach the rhythm and then the notes of Part 3 (bar 3), Part 4 (bar 4), and Part 5 (bars 3–4 and 5–6); really stretch each note to its full value. Sing Parts 3–5 calmly while keeping the swing style intact, and avoid a strict, march-like interpretation.
- Next, sing Parts 3–5 all the way through, making sure the A♭s are in place in Part 5, before putting it all together as a canon. The flattened 3rd, along with the flattened 5th and 7th, are known as blue notes and are used within a key or a chord to create tension. See, e.g., bars 7–10.

▨ Improvising toolbox

- The accompaniment could also serve as a backing for some improvised scat solos. Begin by simply copying the given phrases and then try embellishing them and using them as a springboard for your singers' own ideas. See Part 5 for an example, and try some call and response. Have fun with this and explore the blues!

▨ Listen out

- Make sure Parts 1 and 2 are energized and vibrant. Smile!
- Check that notes are given their full length throughout, and that no one is rushing.

▨ Performing

- This piece was written as a warm up and is not intended for performance, although it could make an effective programme opener. Have fun with it!
- Sing seated or standing, and perhaps add some movement and clicks/claps on the offbeats.
- If you are using the CD backing, sing this piece once through as a five-part canon.

1 Swing Time!

Charles Beale and Steve Milloy

Medium swing ♩ = 112

1 (All voices) — Part 1*
(8) One, two, a one, two, three, four! One, three, one, three,

2 Part 2
(8) Two, four, two, four,

3 Part 3
(8) Shu-be du-bop,

4 Part 4
(8) Shu bop,

5 Part 5
(8) Shu dut dut, du-be du-be du,

Piano — Medium swing ♩ = 112

C nc   C7sus/D A♭/E♭ C7/E   F7

5
(8) one, three, one, three, one, three, one, three,
(8) two, four, two, four, two, four, two, four,
(8) shu-be du-bop, shu-be du-bop,
(8) shu bop, shu bop,
(8) shu dut dut, du yu.___ Shu dut du, du-be du-be du,

B♭9

* Sing each part through in sequence.

Vocal parts, measure 9:

one, three, one, three. Swing time,

two, four, two, four. Swing time,

shu-be du-bop, Swing, time,

shu bop. Swing time,

shu dut dut, du yu. Swing time,

Piano: F9 — C7 — Bb9

Measure 13a:

| 1–4 | | to Part 2 | last time |

Swing time. Now the back-beat. bop bop bop bop ba ba du wah!

Swing time. *Shu - be du - be.* bop bop bop bop ba ba du wah! (to Part 3)

Swing time. Let's Charle-ston! bop bop bop bop ba ba du wah! (to Part 4)

Swing time. Now we're riff - in'! bop bop bop bop ba ba du wah! (to Part 5)

bop bop bop bop ba ba du wah!

Piano chords:
1–4: Fmaj6 Dm7 Gm9 C7
last time: Fmaj6 F7/Eb Bb/D Db7 C7(#5) F F13(#11)

This page may be photocopied

2 You Gotta Move

RESOURCES ▶ CD1 track 2 (performance)

Information

Perhaps known best through the recording by blues guitarist Mississippi Fred McDowell, this spiritual in the African American tradition speaks of hope through change and embodies the spirit of the blues. Sing it as a meditation, or build to a powerful, uplifting climax in the improvised middle section, as on the CD.

Starting

- Look at the words together and ask the singers what the song means to them. Who might need to 'move' and in what way? What is the emotion?
- Stand in a circle and build this rhythm exercise in stages. First, count a slow four beats (c.♩ = 70). Ask the group to clap on the fourth beat only, then add a stamp on the first beat. Finally, add three thigh slaps:

stamp   slap   slap slap   clap

Then, as a group, walk slowly around in a circle, feet in time, stamping, slapping, and clapping the rhythm.
- Still walking around in a circle work on producing a forward, full, rich vocal sound on a low F, using 'mm', 'ng', and 'ah'. Then progress to 'oo', which should be sung with the feeling of a big 'ah' at the back of the throat for resonance. Make sure each member of the group keeps their body moving throughout, to ensure that the vocal energy does not drop.

Teaching and rehearsing

- Teach the chorus by rote, one phrase at a time.
- Next teach the verses in the same way. The opposites ('rich' and 'poor', 'young' and 'old') will help singers to remember the words.
- Say 'gotta' with a soft 't' and use brighter American vowels (e.g. 'gahduh' for 'gotta' and 'cawz' for 'cos').
- The blues style is personal, and the group should sound like individual soloists singing together rather than blend as a 'tight' choir; don't be over-prescriptive about the cut-offs on short phrase endings.
- The slides should sound natural—draw attention to the need to start *under* the note (perhaps a tone), but allow the timing of the slide to happen spontaneously, without forcing it or prescribing a result.

Improvising toolbox

- Ask everyone to sing the riff ('you gotta move') in unison, while keeping the beat going with their feet.
- Now suggest that each person adds their own ideas in the gap. Some singers may feel apprehensive at first; stress that it is fine, indeed helpful, simply to sing the riff, as this will help others keep time and provide an overall structure. You can hear some ideas on the CD; other initial ideas might include:
  - Harmonize 'you gotta move' by singing other pitches, higher or lower than the starting-point.
  - Repeat 'you gotta move' at a different time, or just sing 'move', or 'whoa, yeah', etc. whenever you feel like it. Listen for a space in the texture where nothing is going on and fill it with sound.
  - Join in with a line someone else has made up, or harmonize with it.
  - Think of a rhythm that keeps the groove going and sing it on one note.

Listen out

- Listen out for rhythmic differences between individuals. To encourage a more soloistic group response, you might decide to leave them in, rather than aim for a tighter ensemble.
- Check the tuning of lower notes, and the root (F) especially.
- Make sure the choir is singing 'but when the Lord' in the verses and 'cos when the Lord' in the chorus.

Performing

- Experiment with a range of forms and structures, e.g.:
  - Start with a soloist and bring in everyone gradually.
  - Have the whole group sing verse 1, chorus, verse 2, chorus, and then improvise using the 'you gotta move' riff with the leader bringing back the final verse on cue.
  - Begin with a freely improvised vocal introduction, coming in from nothing or perhaps from a held F. Disappear back to nothing at the end.
  - Try playing the accompaniment vamp initially to support the singers but then drop out, leaving the vocal texture alone.
  - Explore a quiet, meditative version and then a louder, more assertive one.

2 You Gotta Move

Fred McDowell and Gary Davis
arr. Charles Beale

Slow swing shuffle ♩ = 70

Vamp (round and round)   Verse (on cue)

Voices

1. You may be rich, you may be

poor, you may be young, you may be old. But when the Lord

gets rea-dy, you got-ta move.

Chorus

You got-ta move, you got-ta move, you got-ta move,

_ child,   you got-ta   move,   'cos when the Lord _   gets

Bb7   Bo7   F/C   D7

(after v. 2: optionally to riff) [1,2]   last time

rea-dy,   you got-ta move.   2. & 3. You may be   _

G7   C7   F7

Riff   Embellish, and optionally add own parts

repeat ad lib. | last time   to bar 3

You got-ta   move,_   3. You may be

F7

2   You may be high,
    you may be low,
    you may be down,
    no place to go.
    But when the Lord gets ready,
    you gotta move.

3   You may be black,
    you may be white,
    you may be wrong,
    you may be right.
    But when the Lord gets ready,
    you gotta move.

3 Take me to the water

RESOURCES ▶ CD1 track 3 (performance)

Information

This song can be used in worship or in concert. It is, on one level, about baptism: a symbolic contact with water that for Christians symbolizes new life, forgiveness, and the cleansing of sins. Like many African American songs, the words have a double meaning: 'I'm going back home' can refer to the African homeland or any place of freedom from slavery, and also to heaven—a place of comfort, freedom, and spiritual community. This is a gentle, spiritual song which can build, through repetition, to a spectacular and uplifting climax, or finish quietly and with intimacy. Nina Simone first recorded it in 1966 on *Nina Sings Nina* and it is available on a number of compilations. This song works well in unison but can also be sung in three parts or with improvised solos and backings.

Starting

- This is a slow, warm song, so warm up with some humming; focus on creating a resonant sound, with vibrating lips and a loose jaw.
- Sing some slow scales to 'ah' and 'ee', initially just up and down a 5th (Eb–Bb), then perhaps extending up to Eb.
- Finally, change the 'ah' and 'ee' to vowels found in the song. The 'wa-' of 'water', in particular, needs care on the top note (bar 3). Add a touch of 'ah' to brighten the sound and create a big space at the back of the throat.

Teaching and rehearsing

- Start at the beginning, and teach the melody phrase by phrase, in three or possibly four sections. Note that the words repeat and the easiest phrase comes first. Aim for a quiet but energetic sound.
- Next, cover the words to verse 2, still in unison at this stage.
- Decide on a dynamic shape for the song—perhaps a big climax in verse 2 before returning to a quiet final verse, or a big and bombastic finish, with pauses on the final notes ('to', 'be', 'bap-', '-tized') and a final held chord.

Ideas

- Consider refining the arrangement by adding parts. If your choir is less experienced but wants to add some harmonies, sing the first bars in unison, splitting into three parts at the beginning of bar 3. Alternatively, one verse could have harmony throughout. Ensure that each part contains at least one more confident singer to hold the line.
- A soloist, or a number in relay, could sing the first verse, which could then be echoed by the choir. They could also sing the last verse, or just the last line, to bring down the dynamic and emphasize the final mood.
- Try adding some backing 'oo's behind any solo verses, or perhaps behind the last verse. Teach one line initially or all three, depending on the level of your group. Use 'ah' on the louder verses.
- How about a piano-only verse in the middle, as a meditation? Or why not play a solo version of the melody on a recorder, violin, or saxophone?

Improvising toolbox

- In her recording, Nina Simone improvises her own line above the last verse. If you have a soloist, suggest they have a go at doing the same. Ask the soloist to focus on the gaps between phrases, where they will be heard and can sing in question and answer with the group. You could base your version on her words (shown on p. 9) or improvisation, or add your own ideas around 'going home', 'peace in my heart', or anything else you feel fits.
- If your group has learnt the 'oo's, encourage singers to invent their own versions in performance, so that everyone has their own individual backing.

Listen out

- Watch out for a tendency to go flat on the way down the scale at the end of each verse.
- Are the singers singing with energy right through to the end of the line on long notes?
- Listen out for a slight emphasis on the first beat.

Performing

- With this kind of simple repeating song, it is important to be clear about the final form. In some performances it can be appropriate to keep things flexible, so that whoever is leading the group indicates a repetition with a hand signal of some kind. Listen to the CD for an example of this—this was recorded in one take, and you can hear the singers listening to each other and creating a new structure as they work. Alternatively, decide on a definite form, and ensure that everyone in the group knows exactly in which order the various elements happen, so a flexible workshop rehearsal turns into a tight performance.

- Try an initial sing-through of all the verses, building gradually, followed by a verse on the piano and a final quiet verse by a soloist, with 'oo's from other singers behind.
- Before the performance, it is worth reiterating the meaning of the words and the peaceful, spiritual quality of the song.

Background voices

Optional lead line above last verse:

I'm going back home,
Gonna stay here no longer.
I'm going back home
To be baptized.

3 Take me to the water

Slow committed ballad ♩ = 75

Trad., arr. Charles Beale

Lead:
1. Take me to the wa - ter, take me to the
(2.) right - eous, none_ but the

Upper harmony / Lower harmony:
1. Take me to the wa - ter, take me to the
(2.) right - eous, none_ but the

Piano: A♭   E♭

wa - ter, take me to the wa - ter to be bap - tized.   2. None but the
right - eous, none but the right - eous shall be saved.   1. Take me to the

Fine   (*repeat v. 1*)

wa - ter, take me to the wa - ter to be bap - tized.   2. None but the
right - eous, none but the right - eous shall be saved.   1. Take me to the

Piano: B♭7sus   E♭   A♭   E♭/G Fm/A♭ E♭/B♭ B♭7sus   E♭   A♭

Fine   (*repeat v. 1*)

4 My man's gone now

RESOURCES ▶ CD1 track 4 (performance)

Information

Written as part of George Gershwin's 1934 opera *Porgy and Bess*, 'My man's gone now' is a melancholy song sung by a hard-working African American woman (Serena), who loves a man who is never there. Although the pitch range seems wide, it sits well on the voices of less experienced singers, particularly those with lower voices. The song can suit girls, who enjoy exploring the difference between their richer lower register and 'flutier' higher tones. Acting the part is crucial; this is also a jazz song that suits initial exploration of vocal improvising over a very simple repeating riff.

Starting

- Warm up by exploring differences in sonority between higher and lower registers. Begin lower down, singing 'climbin' up the stairs' (bars 11–14) to 'woh-oo woh-oo woh woh' and 'hey-ee ey-ee ey yeah'.
- Now try the 'My man's gone now' phrase lower down—perhaps on E G G E. Work up in semitones to the written pitch once confident. Avoid implying that the C is high!
- Do a story-telling exercise, where singers explain how they felt when something happened (dog died, parent unexpectedly angry, boyfriend or girlfriend left). Ask them to put the story of this song into their own words.

Teaching and rehearsing

- Explain that the form is AAB and teach the whole of the A phrase (bars 5–14). Work on diction and story-telling first. Possibly leave the more chromatic bridge ('Ain't that I mind workin'...') until after the main phrase is in place.
- When you do get to the bridge, teach the pitches by rote as a rising scale, possibly without the written accompaniment.
- Finally, teach the coda. Start with everyone on the top part and gradually add in the other lines, repeating as necessary. Give a clear cue when you are ready to end.

Improvising toolbox

- In the coda, the 'My man's gone now' phrase is repeated in a simple echo formation. Perhaps make a similar canon from one of the phrases of the melody; make up your own phrases and do the same.
- Position your singers around the room in groups of 3–4. Give each group a different line (e.g. 'My man's gone

now' or 'ain't no use a list'nin"). Ask each group to use these words to make up a new repeating melodic line that works over the riff piano chords. Perhaps keep the rhythm the same for security or use the melody from the song. Play the piano chords round and round, while the groups invent lines simultaneously—this can be noisy! Then share the ideas and decide which could go forward to the final performance.

- In a later warm up, teach the minor pentatonic scale of the song to 'ah'.

ah

If you have a younger group, you could teach the scale in two sections:

ah   *ah*

Play Am7 D7 round and round, and ask individuals to sing answers to the musical question 'my man's gone now', sung by the group. Initially, answers might be on one note from the scale and sung to 'la', 'hey', or 'woh'.

Listen out

- Check that the long notes at the ends of phrases are sustained for their full length.
- Is the tone resonant low down? Remind singers not to drop their heads on lower notes.
- Intervals in the bridge melody can need care—use the piano as a reference.
- Make sure that the relatively slow speed stays regular and energized.

Performing

- Could a soloist or small group sing all or part of the song before the whole group joins in?
- This song can work well with groups standing in small groups too, rather than in a conventional 'choir' format.

4 My man's gone now

George Gershwin
arr. Charles Beale

Weary jazz waltz, swing ♩ = 90

1. My man's
2. Ole man

gone now,   ain't no use   a list'n-in'   for his tired__ foot-steps
sor-row's   come to keep   me comp'ny,   whis-per-in'   be-side me__

climb-in' up__ the   stairs._____
when I say__ my   prayers._____

This page may be photocopied

16
Ain't that I mind work-in', work and me is tra-vel-ers jour-ney-in' to -
Eb7sus
Ab6/9
E9sus
Am9
F#9sus
21
last time to Coda
(divide ad lib.)
D.S. al Coda
- ge - ther to the pro-mised land.
Bm9
E7sus
E7+
Am11
Bbmaj7(#11)
Am11
E7+
CODA
My man's gone now,
repeat ad lib.
last time
27
1
2
gone now
(last time tutti)
3
land,
to the pro-mised land.
CODA
Am7
D9
Am7
E7+
repeat ad lib.
last time
Am11
p

5 People get ready

▦ Information

Curtis Mayfield was one of the most accomplished and popular singers of the 1960s and 1970s. Like Stevie Wonder and Marvin Gaye, he combined a vocal style originating in US black churches with a successful career singing pop music. This simple but committed song from 1965 was popular both in and out of the church context, and Mayfield's understated yet conversational approach with The Impressions demonstrates fantastic interpretational creativity around a simple starting-point.

▦ Starting

- This song needs a rich, resonant vocal sound that contains a balance of head and chest voice. Warm up by singing the first two phrases, 'People get ready, there's a train a-comin". Move the starting note up and then down in semitones to cover the range of the group.
- Underlying the melody is the rhythm ♩.♪ ♩𝄾, where the second note is an anticipation of the third beat. Establish a steady crotchet/quarter-note pulse and begin by clapping on beats 1 and 3 and stamping on beats 2 and 4.
- Divide into two groups and—still clapping and stamping—say 'boom, chick, boom, chick', with one group saying 'boom' and the other 'chick':

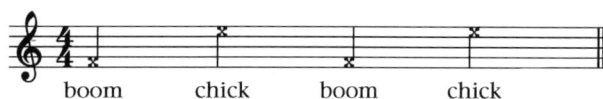

boom   chick   boom   chick

Then move the second 'boom' back one quaver/eighth-note, like this:

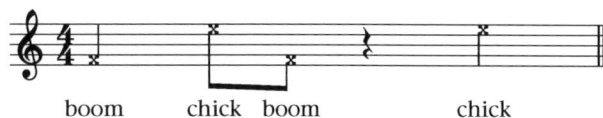

boom   chick boom   chick

If the group is large enough, divide into three groups and add a 'hi-hat' part:

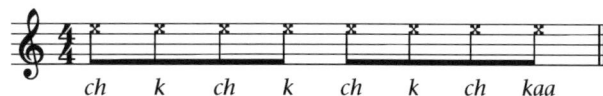

ch   k   ch   k   ch   k   ch   kaa

▦ Teaching and rehearsing

- Begin with the first verse, which could also be a chorus. The words are the hardest part, so learn them first. Start by saying the words to the rhythm on a monotone, keeping the pulse strict. Aim to teach the phrasing at

this point too, by slightly stressing the main syllables and ghosting (or 'unstressing') the rest: i.e., '**Peo**-ple get **rea**-dy, there's a **train** a-**com**-in".
- Now sing the song in a relaxed, almost conversational way, as you would ordinarily speak—initially without singing out or 'performing'. For example, avoid singing through the unstressed note, i.e. 'rea-dy', not 'rea-deeee'. Keep the last notes generally short (but not staccato—just as you would say them), except for 'board' and 'Lord', which can sound fuller and add contrast by being more 'sung'. In bars 8 and 12, the melody sings the lowest of the three notes.
- Try singing verse 1 again, this time adding in the upper and lower harmonies at the ends of phrases.
- Verses 2 and 3 use the same melody, but you'll need to take care with the words to ensure that they fit. Once again, teach the words first, focusing on the rhythm of each phrase and, in particular, on the unstressed syllables, so that the important syllable is stressed on the correct place in the bar.

▦ Improvising toolbox

- Invent other parts to go along with the existing ones. For example, try filling the gaps after each line with a shorter line that uses the same words, e.g. 'People get ready—get ready; there's a train a-comin'—there's a train'.
- All sing the bass-line, then explore adding your own extra pitches over it. Use any sounds you like ('do', 'la', 'ba', etc.) or words from the song. This could turn into its own verse, or be incorporated into the accompaniment between verses.

▦ Ideas

- Set the group the task of making their own arrangement:
  ◦ Add contrast by varying solo and whole-group lines, e.g. 'picking up passengers' (solo), 'coast to coast' (group).
  ◦ Consider going up a semitone (half-step) in the last verse/chorus, or singing or humming the last phrase over the piano ending, as on the CD.
- Invent a simple swaying dance routine. Get ideas by watching videos of black, gospel, and soul groups from the 60s and 70s such as The Impressions, The Four Tops, and The Temptations. Listening to groups such as these is also a great way to learn the inflections of the gospel/soul style.

▢ Listen out

- Make sure the groove is always clear by practising the 'boom, chick' rhythm again once you know the song. Watch out for a tendency to rush, and place all words on the steady quaver/eighth-note subdivision.
- Ensure that the diction stays clear throughout.

▢ Performing

- Vary the arrangement and create pace and drama by adding touches invented by the group in the workshop rehearsals above. Perhaps begin or end with your own version of the introduction, or do an unaccompanied verse.
- If you are using the CD backing, try the following:
    ~ verses 1 to 3, with a piano link between each verse
    ~ piano link, then solos (8 bars)
    ~ piano ending (singers optionally repeat final phrase in last 2 bars).

5 People get ready

Curtis Mayfield
arr. Charles Beale

60s gospel rock ballad; quietly confident ♩ = 75

(Piano introduction)

1. Peo - ple get rea - dy, there's a train a - com - in'. You
2. Peo - ple get rea - dy for the train to Jor - dan.
3. There ain't no room for the hope - less sin - ner who would

don't need no bag - gage, you just get on - board. All you
Pick - ing up pas - sen - gers coast to coast.
hurt all man - kind just to save his own. Have

need is faith to hear the die - sel hum - min'.
Faith is the key, op - en the doors and board them.
pi - ty on those whose chan - ces grow thin - ner, for there's

Don't need no tic - ket you just thank the Lord.
There's hope for all a - mong those loved the most.
no hi - ding place a - gainst the king - dom's throne.

Piano ostinato

60s gospel rock ballad; quietly confident ♩ = 75

© 1966 Mijac Music, USA. This arrangement © 2008 Mijac Music, USA

6 'Deed I Do

RESOURCES ▶ CD1 track 6 (performance); CD2 track 8 (backing)

☐ Information

This resolutely upbeat song was a chart hit in 1927. It has since been sung by many great singers, including Ray Charles, Billie Holiday, Nat 'King' Cole, Blossom Dearie, Marvin Gaye, Bing Crosby, and, most recently, Diana Krall. This arrangement takes advantage of the song's simplicity to create an opportunity for less experienced singers to perform jazz.

☐ Starting

- There are some long notes here, so focus on breathing. Click your fingers at ♩ = 60 and ask the group to do this cyclical routine: inhale for four beats, hold for four, exhale for four, relax for four. Repeat this exercise using five, six, seven, and even eight beats, ensuring that singers inhale and exhale to the full. Try hissing the breath out, pushing from the diaphragm.
- Cover the first two exercises in the 'Starting' section of No. 1 'Swing Time', around an emphasis on beats 2 and 4, and say this 'doo-vah' phrase over the accompaniment. Stress the first 'doo' and the second 'vah', but speaking all four subdivisions:

doo - vah   doo - vah____

Repeat this, but gradually reduce the volume of the two middle syllables or subdivisions, creating 'doo-vah':

doo   vah____

- Insert this rhythm at 'I do' in the ''Deed I do' phrase, feeling the missing subdivisions even though they are not articulated. You can choose whether to sing 'do' as an anticipation (as on the CD) or on the downbeat, as in the score.

☐ Teaching and rehearsing

- Explain that the form is AABA, and start with the 'AA' (bars 3–10).
- Breathing needs care here. You can split the phrase up with a breath before 'Oh my', or do the first four bars in one go. To make the second half of the phrase more emphatic, breathe before 'do I' in bar 6. Your singers should pick this up quickly, so sing it to them and encourage them to join in.

- The first interval on 'Do I?' is a minor 3rd, as is the interval on 'Hon-ey'. Work on creating a resonant tone by singing a bright nasal 'nya' on G E A G E. The phrase begins higher up in the range, but the positive assertion of ''deed I do!' is much lower and needs care. Sing right through to the end of the phrase and ensure that ''deed I do!' has as much energy and resonance as the beginning of the phrase.
- Now move on to bars 11–25. Make sure the 'B' section (bars 11–18) stands out. Try singing it in a quieter, smoother, and more personal way, and make the final 'A' section ('Do I . . .') more extrovert and declamatory. To achieve this, try singing the 'B' section to 'loo' and the 'A' section to 'nya'.
- To develop a resonant sound, you could also try singing the whole melody to 'nya'. Think about singing in ways that keep your sound rounded and full but use those bright 'nya' resonances. Then try the same exercise using 'loo'.

☐ Ideas

- The optional counter-melody is sustained and goes down in steps. You can use it over the final 'A' section for emphasis, and also in the second 'A' if you like.
- To lengthen the arrangement, why not include a short instrumental break, as on the CD? Perhaps the piano could play the 'AA' section and the singers come back in on the 'B' bridge.
- Alternatively, singers or instrumentalists could take it in turns to improvise a melody over the sequence, or simply over a repeating groove, as follows:

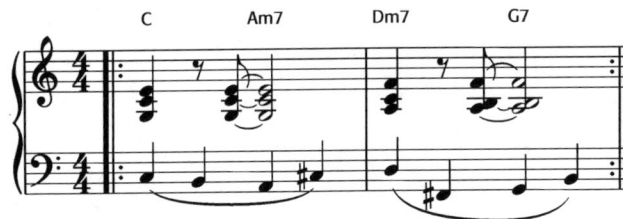

☐ Listen out

- If you use the counter-melody, make sure that both groups of singers listen to each other to ensure that the melody is heard even though it is at a lower pitch.
- Keep the speed absolutely constant, emphasizing the steady crotchet/quarter-note pulse in the piano and avoiding any tendency to rush.

◾ Performing

- In a 'groove' tune like this, it is good to use your body to communicate the pulse and rhythmic energy to the audience. Try tapping a toe or clicking your fingers.
- These songs were intended not only to make their emotional point but also to be upbeat and entertaining. If possible, find a DVD of Frank Sinatra, Nat 'King' Cole, and other vocal groups like The Hi-Lo's. Notice how they smile and use relaxed, open body language. Try to adopt this informal style of performing, perhaps by getting a group member to count the song in, or by suggesting that the audience joins in by clapping or singing towards the end.

6 'Deed I Do

Walter Hirsch and Fred Rose
arr. Charles Beale

20s swing; with a smile! ♩ = 138

Do I_____ want you?___
Do I_____ need you?___

Oh my,___ do I,_____ Hon-ey,___ 'deed I

do! 'deed I do!_____

11
mp
I'm glad that I'm the one who found you,
F
E7
mp
15
that's why I'm al - ways hang - in' 'round you.
A7
D7
G7
19
f
1
Do I love you? Oh my, do I,
(opt. counter-melody)
f
2
ah
C
C7
Fmaj9
Fm6
f

This page may be photocopied

© 1926 and 2008 (arrangement) Stasny-Music Corp, USA, Range Road Music Inc and Quartet Music

last time to Coda
D.S. al Coda
23
Hon-ey, 'deed I do!
Hon-ey, 'deed I do!
C/G A7 D7 G7 C Dm7 G7+
CODA
27
Hon - ey, 'deed I, Hon - ey,
do! 'deed I, Hon - ey,
CODA
C Em7 A7 D7
30
'deed I do!
'deed I do!
G9sus G7 C G7 C
ff

7 Me Ol' Bamboo

RESOURCES ▶CD1 track 7 (performance)
▶ CD2 track 9 (SABar backing) and 10 (SA/TB backing)

Introduction

The Sherman Brothers have given us some of the most 'Supercalifragilisticexpialidocious' music ever written, and this clever, comical patter song from the film *Chitty Chitty Bang Bang* is no exception. The key to this piece is to keep your face relaxed; take quick, deep breaths; and work on diction. It's a great novelty number, and the possibilities for choreography and props are endless! Two arrangements are provided: one for SA or TB voices, and another for SABar mixed choir.

Starting

• Explain that this piece is in a two-beat—or 'boom-chick'—style used in marches, ragtime, vaudeville, country, and even gospel. Establish a pulse of ♩ = 129 and, to a crotchet/quarter-note beat, say 'boom, chick, boom, chick' round and round, creating an accompaniment texture. Play some of the piano part to the group, so they can hear it make the same sound.
• Try the breathing exercises on p. xii to establish good breath support.
• Work towards relaxed and precise diction by singing the 'Popacatapetal' exercise on p. xv.
• Now count '1, 2, 3, 4, 5, 6, 7, oh!', softly at first but connected to the breath and the hissing muscles. Get louder and create more space in the mouth with each run-through until you get to a full shout without tension.

Teaching and rehearsing

• Establish a pulse of ♩ = 100 and sing the melody together slowly on 'dee', starting with the verse and then the chorus. Keep the 'ee' tone bright and focused in the front of the mouth.
• Maintaining a bright tone, add the words of verse 1, and then the chorus, a phrase at a time. Keep your lips relaxed, the diction clean, and the rhythm precise. Speed up a bit with each successful run-through.
• Now add the words for verse 2, which includes a comic spoken solo. There are no rules for how this solo should be performed: ask for some volunteers, and encourage them to have fun with it!
• Now add some parts. Watch the tuning at the end of the chorus phrases; you may need to practise these slowly at first.
• Finally, add bars 5–8 and 37–40 to the choruses, as practised above, and put the whole song together.

Ideas

• Try this song with a cockney accent, as it's sung in the film, as well as with your group's regular accent. Which do you like best? There is no right answer.
• In the film this song is performed in a rather raucous manner! Try using a bright and raucous tone as on the CD, just make sure you don't go overboard!
• Have your group perform web searches for videos of this title. They'll find many versions from amateur productions to perhaps the movie or professional stage version. It's a great place to glean ideas for choreography and staging.

Listen out

• Listen out for the tuning of the opening minor 3rd in the chorus, and the semitone intervals in bars 12 and 15. Try the exercises below:

• Make sure the tone stays bright and the pronunciation clear. Encourage singers to use their mouth/lip muscles and to keep jaws relaxed.

Performing

• The piano part is simple, with fun accents here and there. Make sure it doesn't overpower the singers, and vice versa.
• If you are using choreography, take advantage of the words and the piano accents to make this piece fun for your audience, but don't make the staging so cumbersome that it gets in the way of the singing.
• Don't forget to have fun, and smile throughout!

7 Me Ol' Bamboo

Richard Sherman and Robert Sherman
arr. Steve Milloy

SABar version

Lyrics: Five, four, three, two, one, ho! Here we go! Me

ol' bam-boo, me ol' bam-boo, you bet-ter ne-ver bo-ther with me ol' bam-boo! You c'n

This page may be photocopied

last time **to Coda** ⊕

have me hat or me bum-ber-shoo¹ but you bet-ter ne-ver bo-ther with me ol' bam-boo!

Bb

C7

F7 Bb

unis. *mf*

1. A
2. When

mf

Gm7 Gb7 F7 Bb Gm7 Gb7 F7

mf

Verse 1

gen-tle-man's got a walk-ing stick, a sea-man's got a gaff and the

Bb

F7

mp

¹umbrella

This page may be photocopied

© 1968 Unart Music Corporation and EMI Music Partnership Ltd, USA. Worldwide print rights controlled by Alfred Publishing Co Inc, USA merry men of Robin Hood, they used a quarter staff, on the

Spanish plains, inside their canes, they hide their ruddy swords but

we make do with an ol' bamboo and ev-'ry-one ap-plauds!

Verse 2

This page may be photocopied

52
spear,
Right! But what we do with an ol' bam-boo makes ev - 'ry - bo - dy cheer!
F7
Bb
gliss.
57
(to Chorus)
f
div.
One, two, three, oh! Me
nc
CODA
59
ol' bam - boo!
F9
61
unis. ff
You bet-ter ne-ver bo-ther with me ol' bam-boo!
Bb
Bb7/Ab
Eb/G
Gb7
Bb/F
ff
F7
Bb

7 Me Ol' Bamboo

SA or TB version

Richard Sherman and Robert Sherman
arr. Steve Milloy

Raucous 2-beat! ♩ = 129

Five, four, three, two, one, ho! Here we go! Me ol' bam-boo, me ol' bam-boo, you bet-ter ne-ver bo-ther with me ol' bam-boo! You c'n have me hat or me bum-ber-shoo[1] but you bet-ter ne-ver bo-ther with me ol' bam-boo!

last time **to Coda** ⊕

[1]umbrella

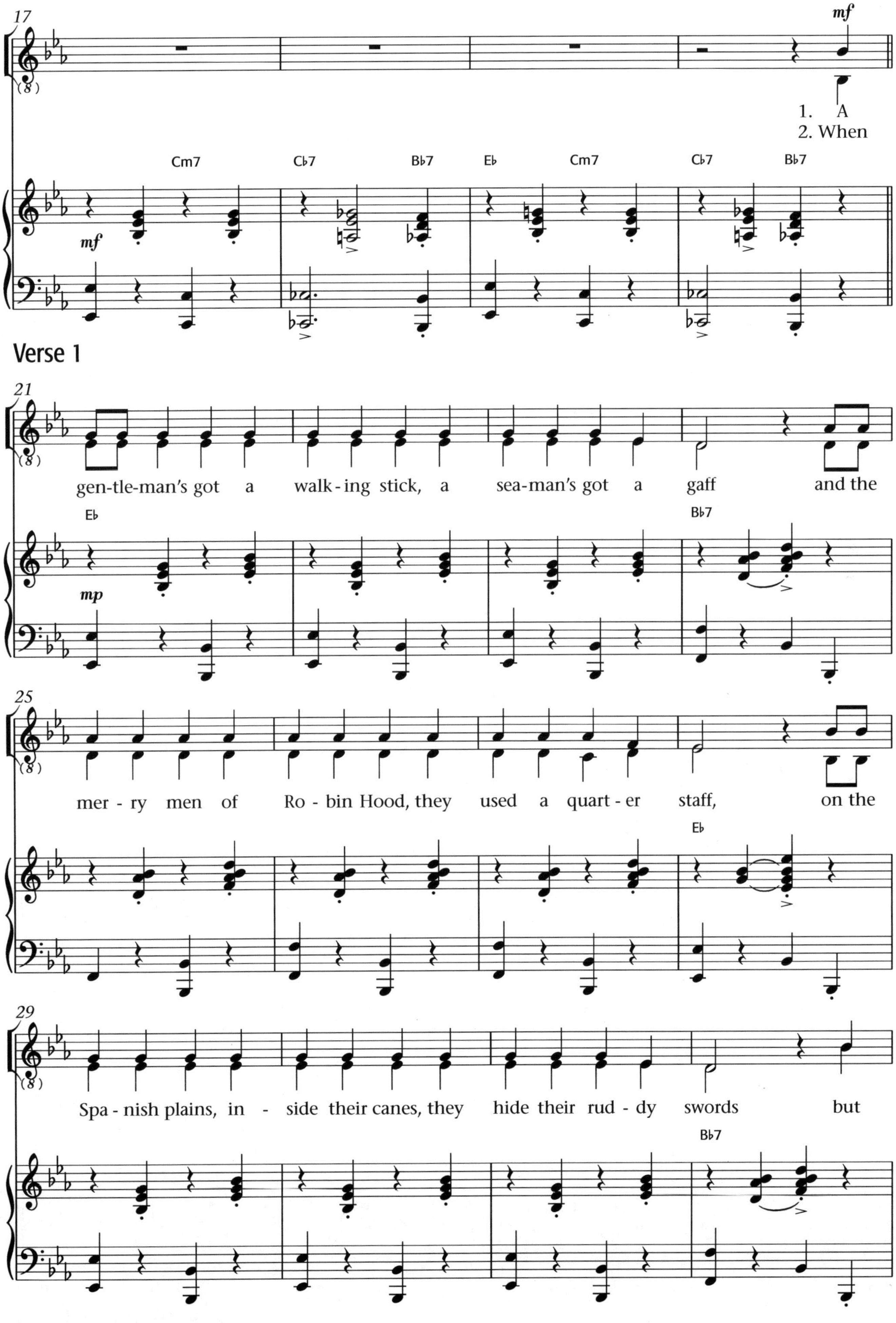

17
mf
1. A
2. When
Cm7 Cb7 Bb7 Eb Cm7 Cb7 Bb7
mf
Verse 1
21
gen-tle-man's got a walk-ing stick, a sea-man's got a gaff and the
Eb Bb7
mp
25
mer-ry men of Ro-bin Hood, they used a quart-er staff, on the
Eb
29
Spa-nish plains, in-side their canes, they hide their rud-dy swords but
Bb7

we make do with an ol' bam-boo and ev-'ry-one ap-plauds!

One, two, three, four, five, six, se-ven, oh! Me

Verse 2

...you use a stur-dy pole,

punt-in' on the beau-ti-ful Thames to pro-

...la-dies use a par-a-sol,

-tect their fair com-plex-ions it's

This page may be photocopied

49
(8)
. . . to have a heft - y spear,
use - ful in the un - der-brush
Right! but
Bb7
53
what we do with an ol' bam - boo makes ev - 'ry - bo - dy cheer!
Eb
gliss.
(to Chorus)
CODA
57
f
One, two, three, oh! Me
nc
59
ol' bam -
Bb7
61
unis.
ff
- boo!
You bet-ter ne-ver bo-ther with me ol' bam-boo!
Eb
Eb7/Db
Ab/C
Cb7
Eb/Bb
Bb7
Eb

8 Little one

RESOURCES ▶ CD1 track 8 (performance)

Information

Have you ever watched someone while they sleep? It can be very moving and peaceful. *Little one* is a gentle lullaby sung to a sleeping child, and it reflects on the dreams that child may be having about their life ahead. In essence, it is a simple melody with a counter-melody later on, but there is also the opportunity for more experienced singers to add their own backings. Although the pitch range is relatively wide, it would suit upper voices well. Most high and low notes are carefully prepared.

Starting

- Practise the underlying ♩ ♪ rhythm by clapping it along with a counted pulse or the piano introduction.
- The melody is often based on a major pentatonic scale:

Sing this sequence to 'ah' and then in different parts of the voice, starting on the B♭ below and the G above, possibly over the opening piano riff in bars 1–2. This will help to get the sound of the song into the singers' ears.

- After an initial sound-based warm up involving humming and breathing (see p. xii), practise a range of vowel sounds from the song, including 'ah' and 'ay', over the introductory piano riff (bars 1–4). Aim for a spacious and resonant sound. e.g.:

ah_____ ay_____

Teaching and rehearsing

- Teach the verses (bars 5–26) in sections first, and then try the outro 'back home' section to set a clear mood. Later in the rehearsal, or even next time, add in the slightly trickier middle section (bars 29–37). Teach the melody to the whole group before adding in the counter-melody.
- Ask your singers to spot repeating melodic shapes. The first two phrases repeat, for example, and others, like 'sleepy eyes' and 'realize', are almost exact repetitions. Focus on differences here; analysing the song in this way will make it easier to learn.

- 'There's a land of flights and fantasy' is the longest phrase. Practise this in a single breath, and sing to the end of the last note.
- Focus on quiet singing in the final section. Keep the pitch up by using the flow of air to maintain the energy through to the end of the phrases, even though they get gradually quieter.

Ideas

- When everyone has learnt the song, try asking each person to sing one line on their own around the group. Could a verse (bars 5–14), both verses (bars 5–26), or the outro conclusion be sung by one person?
- Discuss the musical character and the way each person phrases their line.

Improvising toolbox

- Divide your singers into groups of four or five and position them around the room. Suggest that each group makes up its own riffs to replace or add to the ones given in the outro. Do they need words? Play the piano chords round and round, and when one person has an idea that everyone likes, they should teach it to their group. Write down and/or record the best ideas and try them in different combinations.
- Ask one or two soloists to improvise over the repeating form of the outro, adding the backings later.
- If you have an instrumentalist who can improvise, why not add them too? Use notes from E♭ major for flute and violin, C major for alto saxophone, and F major for clarinet, trumpet, and tenor saxophone.

Listen out

- Check that long notes are counted carefully, e.g. 'one' in 'dreaming of the one some day' (bar 35). The piano part will help your singers to keep in time at certain points by showing where the downbeats are.

Performing

- You could try making the piece longer by going back to the bridge after an outro section that becomes more soloistic.

8 Little one

Charles Beale and Steve Milloy

Childlike, lullaby ♩ = 90

Piano

p

con Ped.

(opt. solo or soli)
unis. p

Lit - tle one, ___ lit - tle one, ___ close your

sleep-y eyes, ___ don't you re-a-lize ___ that

I am here. ___

Work is done,_ you've had time_ for fun, now it's

time for rest,_____ you've done your best,_____ so

S. drift a - way._____

A. drift a - way._____ ah_____

This page may be photocopied

Lyrics under the music:

Can't you see___ there's a land of flights and fan - ta-sy___

ah___ ah___

A♭add2   E♭/G   Cm7   A♭add2   Gm7   Cm11

dream-ing of the one___ some day
dreams can help you find___ your way

ah___

F9(♯11)   B♭13sus

___ you'll be.___
___ back home.___

Back home

B♭sus(♭9)   E♭add2   Cm11   E♭add2

This page may be photocopied

9 Take Me to the Funk!

RESOURCES ▶ CD1 track 9 (performance); CD2 track 11 (backing)

Information

This song was written in tribute to James Brown, Aretha Franklin, Otis Redding, Etta James, and all the 'godfathers and godmothers' of 1960s funk. Funk is an African American musical style that originated in the mid- to late 1960s and blended soul music, soul jazz, and R&B into a new, danceable, groove-oriented form. In this style of music, the rhythm section (guitar, bass, and drums) sets up a syncopated groove that singers can solo over. The harmonic structure is simple and relies heavily on the flattened 3rd and 7th.

Starting

- Try singing the following with a round, bright tone.

- Sing it again, but this time include a small smear on the first note of each phrase, and a large smear on the fourth note. The smear is commonly used in all types of popular music but should be used with care. Enter the note from at least a whole tone below and slide to the written pitch. The longer the note, the more time you may take to smear the pitch.
- Try adding a slightly nasal tone to give the sound an 'edge'.
- The following example introduces the internal groove for this song. Divide your singers into two groups and establish a pulse of ♩ = 85. Have the whole group click on beats 2 and 4, and then add in the hi-hat part, followed by the drum part. Gradually work up to ♩ =116.

Teaching and rehearsing

- Say together the lyrics to the chorus (bars 18–26), vocally acting them as you do so. Add the notes, starting with the melody, and then the backing vocals.
- The singing should be relaxed but 'on the beat' and energized, with a nasal tone if you can.
- The vocal smears are written as grace notes. Smear the grace notes into the following pitch.
- Now teach the two backing vocal parts at bars 27–8. When these are learnt, divide into three groups and put together the whole chorus with some piano accompaniment. Be sure to maintain the difference between the G♮ in the melody and the G♯ in the backing.
- Now teach the verses in the same way.

Ideas

- Try using a soloist in one or both verses, and give them the freedom to stray away from the written line. Listen to verse 2 on the CD for an example.
- Find a recording of 'Dance to the Music' by Sly and the Family Stone, and pick out the unaccompanied vocal 'breakdown' (an abrupt change in rhythm or instrumentation). Incorporate your own 'breakdown' after bar 26b. Try starting with the drum-beat exercise above, then adding in the backing vocals part by part, followed by the piano, and then the lead; then sing through to the end.
- Try 'I Feel Good' by James Brown and Christina Aguilera's 'Ain't No Other Man' for examples of this style.
- Find choreography ideas on the Internet (try videos by Ike and Tina Turner, Wilson Pickett, 'Taxman' by the Beatles, 'Miss You' by the Rolling Stones, and 'Run and Tell That' from Hairspray).

Listen out

- Be sure that diction is clear and words are fully understandable.
- Keep the tone bright. If you're using a nasal tone, experiment with the amount to see what is right for you (listen to the above singers for reference).
- Make sure you get to the destination pitch of a smear, even if you decide to arrive just before the next pitch. If you don't, it may sound as if you are singing flat.

Performing

- This song is all about enjoying music, so sing it as such!
- Consider starting with the group positioned together, then having each backing part breakaway as their part enters. A great example of this—both musically and in terms of staging—is 'Dancin'' from the movie Xanadu.

9 Take Me to the Funk!

Words: John Moysen
Music: Steve Milloy

Medium fast funk ♩ = 132

Voices / Piano

(2nd time)

1. When

I'm feel - in' blue,___ I know just what to do: I
(2.) don't need no booze_ to help me lose my blues, a

take a bath and end up feel-in'___ fine. I fix up my hair_ an'
groov-in' li - dl club will do just___ fine. I don't need no drug when

This page may be photocopied

Lyrics (measure 8):
find a top to wear, call up a friend to meet a-round___ nine. Now,
I can cut a rug,[1] just let me hear the band and I'll___ shine. The

E7   A7

Lyrics (measure 11):
I don't need no pills to cure me of my ills, I on-ly need to hear a funk-y___
drum-mer's real-ly cool, ya can't call him a fool, with sax-o-phone, guit-ar-ist and a___

E7   A7   E7   A7

Lyrics (measure 14):
___ beat. When I get the blues I grab my danc-in' shoes an'
___ horn. If I hear a bass, then man, I'm off my face and

E7   A7

Chorus
1st time: all voices
2nd time: Lead

Lyrics (measure 17):
find a place where I can move my feet. Take me to the
I can keep on mov-in' till the dawn!

E7(#9)   B7+   G   A

[1]get down and dance

This page may be photocopied

27
Lead
(4th time only)
x 4
Take me to the
Backing vocals
1
Play that mus - ic real funk - ay.
2
(3rd & 4th times only)
Like my mus - ic so funk - ay.
E7
A7

29
funk,
let me do my thang.
Play that mus-ic real funk - ay.
Play that mus-ic real funk-
Like my mus-ic so funk - ay.
Like my mus-ic so funk-
E7
A7
E7
A7

Take me to the funk, I just got-ta dance

- ay.__ Play that mus-ic real funk - ay.__

- ay.__ Like my mus-ic so funk - ay.__

E7   A7

__ an'__ sing! Take me to the funk, y'all.

Dance an' sing! Take me to the funk, y'all.

Dance an' sing! Take me to the funk, y'all.

E7   B7+   E7

This page may be photocopied

10 This little light of mine

RESOURCES ▶ CD1 track 10 (performance); CD2 track 12 (backing)

▦ Information

This well-known American spiritual is a joyful expression of belief in oneself. During the 1950s and 60s it became known throughout the US as a Civil Rights anthem. Here, we set it in a choral gospel style. You can sing this song in unison, parts, or a mixture of both, and it is ideal for a concert performance or worship service. Your singers will pick this up quickly, so focus on creating a big open sound and a confident performance.

▦ Starting

- Good posture is essential in creating the big sound needed for this piece, so start with some physical warm ups. Use the 'big face, little face' exercise (p. x) to energize the face. Open eyes wide and rub temples, cheeks, nose, and all around the eyes.
- Now tilt your head forward; imagine that the top of your head is a pencil, and on top of that rests a piece of paper. Draw figure of eights on to the paper, side to side, to loosen the neck. Finally, use other stretches (see p. x, 'Posture') to prepare the rest of the body for singing.
- Warm up over the range of this piece by singing the following with a bright, full, energized tone.

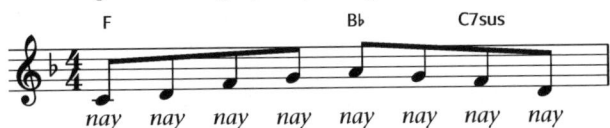

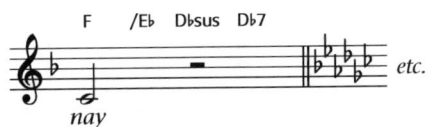

nay nay nay nay nay nay nay nay

nay *etc.*

- Establish a tempo of ♩ = 152 and have the group click on beats 2 and 4. Sing this drum-kit exercise together to internalize the groove; swing the quavers!

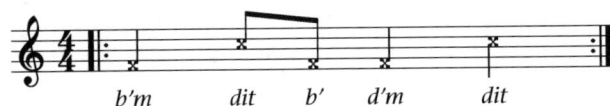

b'm *dit* *b'* *d'm* *dit*

▦ Teaching and rehearsing

- Singing unaccompanied, use call and response to teach the song phrase by phrase, starting with the melody. Add some claps or clicks on beats 2 and 4, and smile!
- If you are singing the three-part arrangement, move on to Parts 2 and 3 and teach them in the same way.
- For a more authentic sound, keep the sound bright and full but try singing with a slightly nasal tone.

▦ Ideas

- Ask a soloist to sing 'This little light of mine', or a lyric they have created, and have the group answer with 'I'm gonna let it shine'.
- If you have a confident soloist, they could ad lib. on the long notes. e.g.:

I'm gon-na let it shine, (glo - ry, hal-le-lu-jah!)

- Along with offbeat clicks or claps, try adding some movement: standing with feet together, step to the right with your right foot on beat 1, and on beat 3 step to the right with your left foot, bringing your feet together. In the next bar, step to the left with your left foot on beat 1, and on beat 3 step to the left with your right foot, bringing your feet together. Start this move in bar 2 and repeat until the tempo change in bar 42. This is known as a 'step-touch' or 'step-together' and is used quite frequently in popular choral styles.

▦ Listen out

- Take care over the 's' at the end of 'This': concentrate on the vowel.
- If the long notes start to lose energy and focus, try incorporating a slight crescendo.

▦ Performing

- Perhaps start with a free-tempo unaccompanied verse before beginning the written arrangement.
- You might try the first verse in unison and add parts for the remaining verses.
- This song is all about pride in one's self no matter what. Make sure your singers' posture and faces convey this!

10 This little light of mine

Spiritual
arr. Steve Milloy

1. This lit-tle light of mine, I'm gon-na let it shine.
2. Ev - 'ry - where I go,— I'm gon-na let it shine.

This lit-tle light of mine,_ I'm gon-na let it shine.
Ev - 'ry - where I go,— I'm gon-na let it shine.

This page may be photocopied

14
This lit-tle light of mine,
Ev - 'ry - where I go,
I'm gon-na let it shine. Let it shine,
I'm gon-na let it shine. Let it shine,
F Bb7/C F Bbmaj6 F/C A7(b9)/C# Dm G9
18
let it shine, let it shine!
let it shine, let it shine!
F/C D7(#9) Gm7 C7 F7 Bb7
1
2
F7 F7 D7sus
22
f
Je - sus gave it to me,
I'm gon-na let it shine.
G7 C7/D G D9sus G D9sus G G7

Je - sus_ gave it to me,___ I'm gon-na let it shine.

C   G9sus   C   G9sus   C   G

Je - sus_ gave it to me,___ I'm gon-na let it shine.

G   C7/D   G   Cmaj6   G/D   B7(♭9)/D♯   Em

___ Let it shine, let it shine, let it shine.

A9   G/D   E7(♯9)   Am7   D7   Em

This page may be photocopied

straight 8ths/quavers
slow down to the end

Let it shine, let it shine, let it shine.

Let it shine,_ let it shine,

let it shine!_____

11 Gitika

RESOURCES ▶ CD1 track 11 (performance); CD2 track 13 (backing)

☐ Information

Gitika (or Gitaka) is a Sanskrit word that can mean 'little song' or 'ballad'; it is also a girl's name. This song is influenced by the jazz fusion and rock music of the 1970s and bands such as Weather Report and Chick Corea's 'Return to Forever'. In particular, this song was inspired by some of the early work of percussionist Airto Moreira and singer Flora Purim, who were developing a particular kind of folk-style Brazilian jazz on albums like *Seeds on the Ground*. The vocal quality they achieved has a timeless beauty about it, though a lot of the lines were incredibly simple.

☐ Starting

- This song is an exercise in sustaining a long note and keeping the energy going right to the end. Warm-up priorities are therefore breathing and resonance.
- Stretch straight up with arms above heads and fingers pointing to the ceiling. Inhale as you lean back slightly and feel the diaphragm working; then exhale and lean slightly forward.
- Bring the arms down but ensure the rib-cage remains raised to allow a good space for the air. Breathe in deeply and gently blow out an imaginary candle in front of your face. Repeat, but now blow harder as though the candle did not go out the first time. Notice the pressure from below.
- Breathe in again, and this time exhale to 'ss', then 'ff', 'vv', and 'mm'. Once the 'mm' is in place, change to 'ng' (as in 'sing'), 'ah', and 'hey-aa', which will throw the sound up into the face.

☐ Teaching and rehearsing

- Teach both halves of the song in order, phrase by phrase. Make sure the song starts quietly, and returns to the quiet mood at the beginning of each round.
- To start with, clap the rhythm of the second half (bars 13–18); then say it, and finally put the pitches to the rhythm.
- The syllables used all contain distinctive vowels. Work on 'hey', 'ah', and 'yo' once the shape is in place, so that all three are strong and well-blended across the group.
- Teach the coda separately, and work on getting the pauses together.

☐ Ideas

- The optional second part is almost in canon with the melody. Divide the group in half and listen to the canon play out.
- Add optional harmonies a 3rd, 4th, or 6th above or below the written part as your group's experience allows. Because much of this piece is modal, you can explore a range of options here.
- Try adding some instrumental parts using, e.g., keyboards or tuned percussion, since the melody is based on the white notes of the keyboard starting on D, i.e. D Dorian, even though the key signature implies D minor. Try exploring D Dorian and D minor pentatonic in your improvising.

☐ Improvising toolbox

- Three rhythms are given below the score. Choose one and use it to invent a repeating pattern that you can sing over the chords in bars 5–12. Will two of those rhythms fit together in a question and answer pattern?
- Invent more melodic phrases by trying different pitch combinations with the given rhythms. Try phrases that move stepwise and others that jump about; phrases that rise and phrases that fall; and phrases that fit smoothly within the harmony, and others that contain melodic surprises.

☐ Listen out

- Check the tuning of the 'yo' on E in bar 7 (and bar 8 in the counter-melody); ensure it does not go down too low.
- Is the rhythm of the second section really crisp? Voices can sometimes get lazy and sing behind the beat when the music is smooth.
- Ensure the long notes stay energized right to the end.

☐ Performing

- In performance, this song needs well-blended and sustained singing. It is ideal for a big resonant space, where the sound can develop a 'bloom'.
- To set the scene, consider adding a slow opening of bars 5–12 without pulse, on sustained Gm11 and Dm11 chords in the piano; then bring in the piano groove from the start, as marked.
- The piece can be repeated several times in performance. There is room for individual solos, backed by the workshop riffs given or others you invent.

11 Gitika

Charles Beale

Medium samba; quietly expressive ♩ = 92

first time: all voices *p*

Hey —

Medium samba; quietly expressive ♩ = 92

Piano

p

Dm

Dm7

5

yah _____ Hey — yo _____ Hey —

2nd time only *p*

Hey — yah _____ Hey — yo _____

Gm7

Dm9

This page may be photocopied

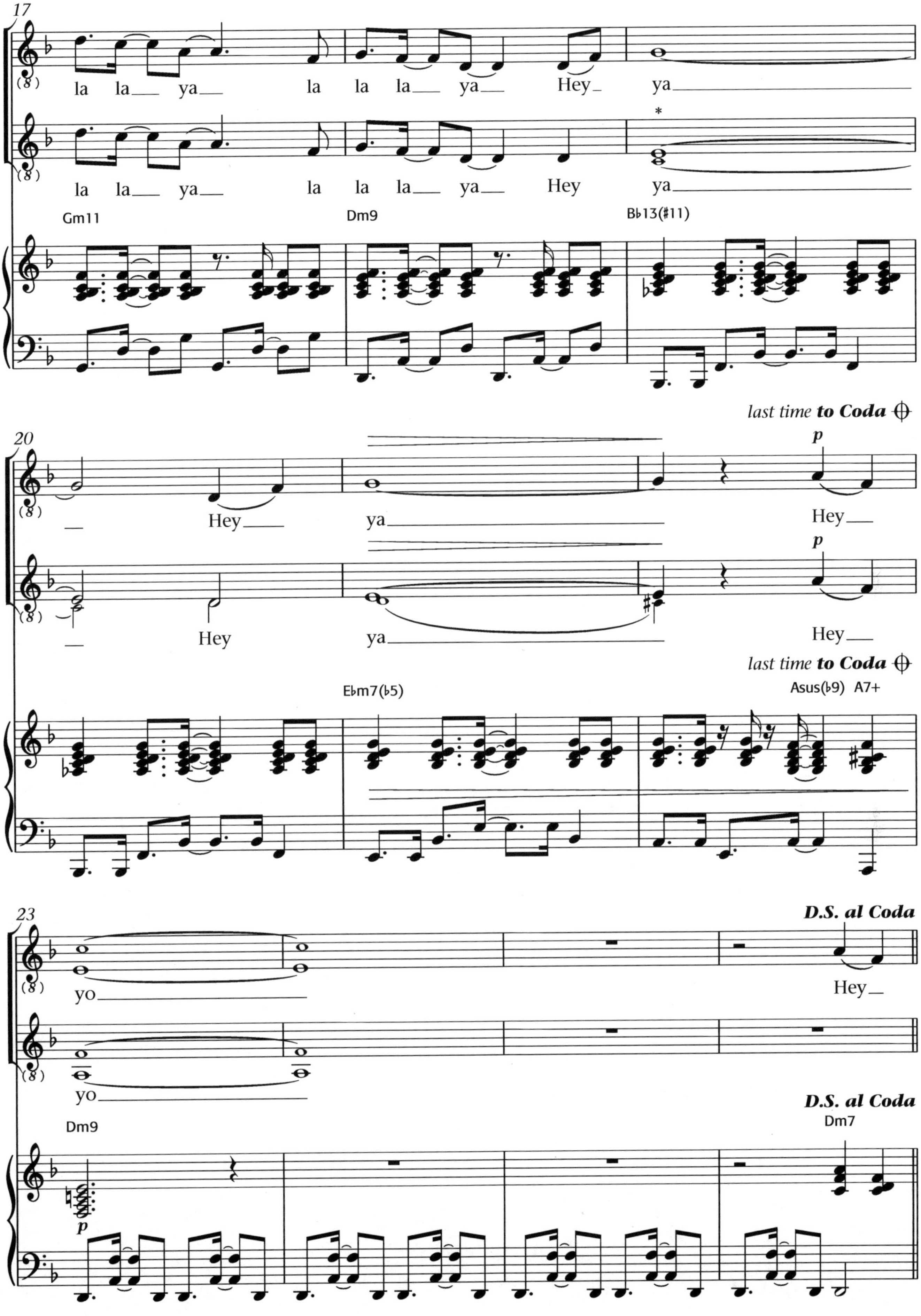

* all small notes optional

Workshop rhythms

bah   bah   dah   bah-dup   bah-dah dup   dee-yah dee-yah

Section II

Moving On

▢ Introduction and practical exercises

Section II builds on the basic advice about good singing covered in 'Preparing to Sing' and Section I and adds in the new element of musical style. This introduction explores the most common and accessible approaches to the voice found specifically in pop, soul, gospel, jazz, and show songs, and these are followed through in the Section II workshops. Rather than develop only one approach, the aim is to increase your singers' vocal flexibility and to enable them to sing with authenticity across a range of musical contexts within the popular field. We begin with some key concepts, introduced through practical exercises.

Breathing

The breath is the foundation of our singing. Continue to work with the exercises in 'Preparing to Sing' (p. xii); here are two more to take your group further:

- Stand tall and relaxed, feet shoulder-width apart, knees relaxed, spine elongated, neck relaxed, and head slightly tilted down. With your lips pursed, sip in air as if sucking through a straw. Start in the chest, expanding the rib-cage and taking in air all the way down to the waist, expanding it to the lower back and through the stomach. Hold for four to eight beats, then pant like a thirsty dog, keeping the throat open and the rib-cage and lower back/waist expanded.
- Take in another cup of air. Hold; pant; then hiss it out slowly, keeping the cheeks high ('inner smile'), the throat open, and the rib-cage and the lower back/waist expanded. Release.
- This time take a full breath and hiss it out. Hiss solidly for four beats, and release; then eight, etc.
- Now hiss solidly for eight beats a couple of times, then cut the length of the hiss in half and do that twice. Keep cutting the length in half all the way down to quavers. Feel the connection to the 'hissing' muscles.

Creating the space for good resonance

Singing requires just a little more space in our mouths. But how much?

- Ask your singers to place a finger just in front of the fleshy nodule that covers their ear.
- Yawn, focusing on what happens to the skin and bone under the finger. Discuss what happens to the finger. They should have felt the bone give way, letting the finger fall in slightly. Now yawn again, focusing on what happens at the back of the roof of the mouth. They should feel a slight lift in the fleshy part (the soft palate), allowing more space for sound to resonate in.
- Yawn again, but this time create only a small indentation or pit underneath your finger. Then sigh, keeping the small indentation and the back of the roof of the mouth slightly

lifted. This gives the right amount of space to sing well in most contexts.

Using your face: your head is an important resonator in singing—a bit like an on-board speaker in a stereo system. So what you do with your face—your lips, tongue, jaw, and the various structures inside your mouth—makes a huge difference to the colour of the sound and its resonance. When singing well, it can feel as though your face is tingling from resonance and air. As well as having a pleasant face for your audience (although that's reason enough!), you will also want your group's eyes to look alive, with cheek-bones slightly lifted—this aids in space as well as resonance.

This exercise aims to get the different parts of the face into a good singing position.

- Say 'Hey!' in a relaxed, bright voice, as though greeting a friend some distance away.
- Rounded lips help your tone and projection—think of your lips as your own personal megaphone. Begin by making a smiley face with closed lips, bright eyes, and a feeling of high cheek-bones.
- Next, bring your lips to a tight pucker, keeping the smile, eyes, and high cheek-bones intact. Slowly open your lips, keeping the corners of the lips inward. Holding it all together, say 'Hey!' again. Release. Discuss how that sounded. How did it feel in your face? Everyone's face is structured differently so it will take each singer time to refine this exercise to suit the structure of their own head's resonant spaces.
- This is an extreme version of what singers do all the time. Make a more relaxed version of that face, and sing something simple on an 'oh' vowel. Play with this in each piece you sing, aiming to use lips, eyes, and cheek-bones to increase the resonance of your sound.

Yawn and sigh: further back in your head is another set of resonators, which you use when you yawn and sigh. This exercise will make you more aware of those spaces inside and will also help you to expand pitch range and get a unified sound across the top and bottom of your register.

- Yawn and relax. Now yawn again, focusing on what happens inside your mouth. Can you feel the fleshy structure at the top of your mouth (the soft palate) rise, making a big space? What happens outside, to your lips and nose? Do they rise up too?
- Begin to yawn and, before completion, just sigh. Repeat again, but this time sigh on 'oo' or 'uh', starting in a high register and sighing downward. Maintain a smooth transition from the yawn to the releasing of sound and keep the lips relaxed.

(Have a good) cry

'Crying' is a sound used by pop singers through the generations, from 50s doo-wop and cabaret crooners up to the Bee Gees or Christina Aguilera. 'Crying' can help you make a 'buzz' or resonance. Frankie Valli used this technique a lot.

- Starting in a high register, on the sound 'wa' (as in 'bat'), imitate a baby's cry. Then sigh on this vowel, maintaining the same tone colour (also known as a 'cry').
- Now, while 'crying' on 'wa', sing the pitches 54321:

- Stay relaxed and open as you go higher by half-step increments, focusing on creating the 'cry' sound in different parts of the voice. You'll be surprised at how high you can go and how easy it is to sing through the vocal registers without manipulation.

- Using the same pitches and tone colour, make a short 'ha' sound, descending in half-step increments.
- Try singing a song with various degrees of 'cry'. Try the solo part of No. 21 'I'm Not Your Pet', or No. 20 'Don't Let the Door Hitcha'.

Fry (it up), mix (it up)

The vocal 'fry' is used to engage sound, and involves producing the lowest sound you can.

- Form your lips into an 'oh' and take a cool, focused breath. Take note of the space it creates as it travels down into your chest—remember this feeling. Release.
- Repeat, then exhale on a low, relaxed, gravelly 'uh', maintaining the chest cavity. This may remind you of the sound your make when you're ill or first wake up.

'Mix' voice may be substituted for 'belt' (see below). This technique mixes the resonances of the head and chest voice to create an even sound through the high and low registers, giving a bigger palate of colours. Add depth in the cavity (as for 'fry', above) for an edgier or brass-like sound in your higher range:

- Do the vocal 'fry' exercise then hold the 'uh' and slide up (like a siren) to the top of your range, maintaining the chest cavity. You may find that the sound gets thinner as your ascend. Let it happen. Try this a few times, working on maintaining the siren without breaks.
- Try sliding to and holding specific pitches all over the range, varying the depth of the chest cavity. Less depth will produce a headier mix.
- When singing with a chestier mix in higher registers (with more depth in the chest cavity), some vowels will need modification—usually towards a taller, more centralized vowel. E.g. 'hair' modifies towards 'here'.

Belt

The 'belt' is essentially a well produced, well supported bright yell, with ideally no tension in the voice. From Broadway and West End singers to pop divas, and rock 'n' rollers to gospel and rhythm 'n' blues singers, 'belt' is the sound used for producing raw emotion in a healthy way. There are whole books written on 'the belt pop sound', and 'belt' is seen as controversial in some voice circles. It certainly needs to be handled with care, to avoid strain. Nevertheless, the 'belt' sound is everywhere in the pop world, and many younger singers use it, so we feel it is important to include a starting-point for doing a 'belt' safely.

- Begin by doing a 'cry' as before, to 'wa', sliding downward for at least an octave. This time, open the back of the mouth and take a deep breath, feeling the connection to the body. Keep the lips relaxed. The sound is fuller and brighter and can carry a long distance.
- Repeat using 'hey' on a mid-range pitch, ascending in half-step increments. Keep it open and relaxed at all times.

You may find this sound becomes harder to produce as you ascend. To avoid strain, go back to a pure 'cry' and then open the back of the mouth gradually. Always stop if you feel any strain or discomfort.

Vowel modification

Some vowels are not suitable for 'belting' because they rest too far back in the mouth or throat. The solution is to modify the vowel—e.g. an 'oo' vowel as in 'moon' could be mixed with the vowel sound in the word 'took' to get a brighter sound. Try this exercise:

- Begin by singing the first two phrases of the chorus of No. 2 'You Gotta Move'. Ascend in half-step increments. The 'oo' vowel becomes harder to sing as you go higher. Try modifying it by mixing in some 'oo' as in 'took'. The space is narrower at the front and the tongue comes forward a bit. Now go higher still, and you'll find this becomes hard too. Now try using 'ah', effectively creating 'marve'. You should find this easier.

There are two considerations when modifying vowels. First, is production of tone easy and comfortable in the brighter resonance you need? And second, can the words still be understood by your listeners? The workshops that follow suggest specific places where you can apply this technique of modifying vowels on a 'belt' to make the sound richer and more engaged, particularly on higher notes. Here are some guidelines:

- 'Ah' (father) and the vowel sound in 'paid' never modify.
- The vowel sound in 'took' stays the same in the low- to mid-range then mixes with 'ah' in the higher range.
- Any 'aw' (paw), 'ah' (Charles), or 'uh' (but) sounds tend to become 'ah'.
- Any 'ee' (need), 'ih' (sit), 'eh' (pet) sounds, or the vowel sound in 'pant', would be mixed with the vowel sound in 'paid', adding in more modifier as it goes higher in the range.
- Any 'oo' as in 'moon' sounds would be mixed with the vowel sound in 'took' in the mid- to beginning-high range, mixing with 'ah' in the higher range.
- 'Oh' (so) stays the same in the lower range, mixes with 'ah' in the mid-range, and then changes to 'ah' in the higher range.

Of course, these are only guidelines. Singers should make their own judgments as to when to use these and whether they work in the musical context concerned. It is also important that a group's vowels blend well, so discuss and come to a common view with your choir.

Vibrato

Vibrato is a very personal issue. Many people say it is natural to all singing, but this is not universally accepted. What we can say is that it varies from style to style as to how much vibrato to use and when to use it. In some jazz and pop styles, as in much Renaissance music, a centralized, minimal (some would say non-existent) vibrato is conventional. An MGM movie or Broadway chorus, however, will tend to have a wider, faster, and more prominent vibrato. Many pop and some stage singers will delay or use less vibrato until the ends of phrases or on long notes within a phrase. In pop or jazz charts using chords with extended harmony, minimized vibrato is essential for tuning purposes and helps make the chord resonate. By contrast, in spirituals/gospel, some standards, and pop, rock 'n' roll, rhythm 'n' blues, etc. more vibrato can be used throughout the phrase. In the following workshops we indicate ways of using vibrato that are central to interpreting the style with authenticity. You will need to adapt them to the needs of your group and ensure they feel comfortable.

Taste and style

The Section II workshops give you many suggestions about singing well in general, and also about groove, tone quality and resonance, and other aspects of style from how to stand to the character of the music. For example, we talk about what should be sung with a 'cry', a 'belt', a normal singing voice, or a mix of these. In the end, these are just suggestions. Your group needs to experiment and play with each song, each phrase—even each word—and then see what works for you. You might decide to 'belt' one phrase and croon the next, using a bit of the 'cry' to engage the sound for a warm buzzing sound, or maybe go for something warmer. Let the music, style, and above all the abilities and enthusiasms of your singers be your guide. Enjoy your singing!

12 He's gone away

RESOURCES ▶ CD1 track 12 (performance)

Information

This is a traditional American song, made famous by singers including Carl Sandburg and Jo Stafford, about someone setting off on a long journey and the doubts of those left behind. It is a wonderfully sad song, in which the words of verse 2 show a clear development in the singer's feelings from fear of what might happen to resignation to what *will*. There is no vocal arrangement here as such, as the group or soloist should use the ideas given here to invent their own. This workshop focuses on developing the group's range of vocal and musical resources, enabling them to project the song's strong emotional content.

Starting

- After some initial stretching and breathing, have the group hum from E to the highest note they can, and then back; now hum to the lowest, and back. Do the same thing then to 'ng', 'aw', and finally 'ah'. Ask each person to choose their own vowel sound. Listen to the range produced and imitate the best ones.
- Play an E major chord. Have singers collectively, but in their own time, sing up and down an E major arpeggio as high and low as is comfortable. Then each sing a single note over the E chord—some will choose 1, some 3, and some 5—and experiment with the balance and spacing of the chord.
- Learn the final phrase of the song (bars 15–18), which will later form the basis of the improvised section. Staying with this phrase, play the chords on the piano and ask each singer to start on a note of their choice from the E chord, singing to 'ah'. As the chords change, encourage each person to sing their own line to create instant harmony, moving up and down or staying put as they choose.

Teaching and rehearsing

- Begin by teaching the words alone by rote, so singers get the sense of the structure.
- Next, having already learnt the last phrase, work through the song phrase by phrase from the beginning. Teach the dynamics and expressive details straightaway, to make the learning process more interesting and musical. The aim is for everyone to sing in unison exactly together.
- Sing the song directly to your singers and ask them to sing it back exactly as you sing it. If you sing quietly, they should too, and so on. Use a keyboard or other pitched instrument for support as needed.
- Check the song is learnt by asking each singer (or group of five or six singers, if you have a large group) to sing a line one by one, so the song is sung in sections by a series of individuals. Repeat with a different person or group starting, so everyone sings a different part of the song the second and third times. This is also a good way of enabling (and discovering) singers who might want to sing a solo.

Improvising toolbox

- Ask everyone to sing the last phrase together, then sing it again with everyone adding their own ideas. Make clear that it is fine simply to sing the melody again. You will hear singers begin to explore their own ideas, but some will take longer than others. Repeat the exercise, giving singers a chance to rehearse and refine their ideas and gradually gain confidence.
- Teach one group to sing the piano bass-line against the melody, and suggest that everyone works around that, perhaps giving some starting-point lines for them to sing.
- How can you tell when to bring an improvised section to a close? As you listen, you will hear individuals making their marks and should follow your gut feeling about when to encourage by nodding, smiling, and indicating you want more, and when to return to the tune. Your job is to lead the singers towards a more interesting performance, and to allow them to express themselves.

Ideas

- As the rehearsal/improvised exploration continues, elements of a possible form will appear. Perhaps begin by singing together in unison. After a period in the middle where something else happens (a solo, an improvised section, some predefined backings), end by singing the song again—perhaps quieter, or in another way which suggests the performance has been on a journey.
- Choose the best ideas, praise them, and capture them in the final arrangement. Was there a particularly good soloist who could start off the song? Could some people sing backing 'oo's over the piano chords? Would a freely improvised unaccompanied introduction set the mood?
- It can be useful to record a performance at the end of a workshop and/or to make written notes, so at the next rehearsal you carry on from the same place.

- Ensure everyone is clear about the song's emotional content—what it actually means—as this will add power to the final performance. Discuss the words, asking 'Do they have a special meaning for anyone here?', and see if anyone has a personal story they want to share. This feeling of shared meaning around a song can create spellbinding musical results and motivation for creative endeavour.

Listen out

- Good ensemble is important in vocal improvising of this kind. Is anyone sticking out? Can everyone hear the less confident singers too?
- If someone is singing a solo, is the rest of the group responding by sinking slightly into the background?
- Do the dynamics come up and down as the group sings? The group should be responding to one another, so as a soloist gets louder or softer, everyone else follows.

Performing

- It is crucial that everyone can hear everyone else. Stand appropriately, perhaps in a slight circle or a block.
- Ensure that the elements of your structure are absolutely clear. Do you need an introduction (a chord, or perhaps the first or last few bars of the melody)? How many times does the melody go round? What is the end, and how is it cued? If an improvisation is going well, what happens next? Are there harmonies that have become fixed during the improvising and that everyone should now know?

12 He's gone away

Trad.
arr. Charles Beale

Slowly, colla voce, with intensity ♩ = 72

He's gone a-way for a stay a lit-tle while, but he's com-ing back if he

This page may be photocopied

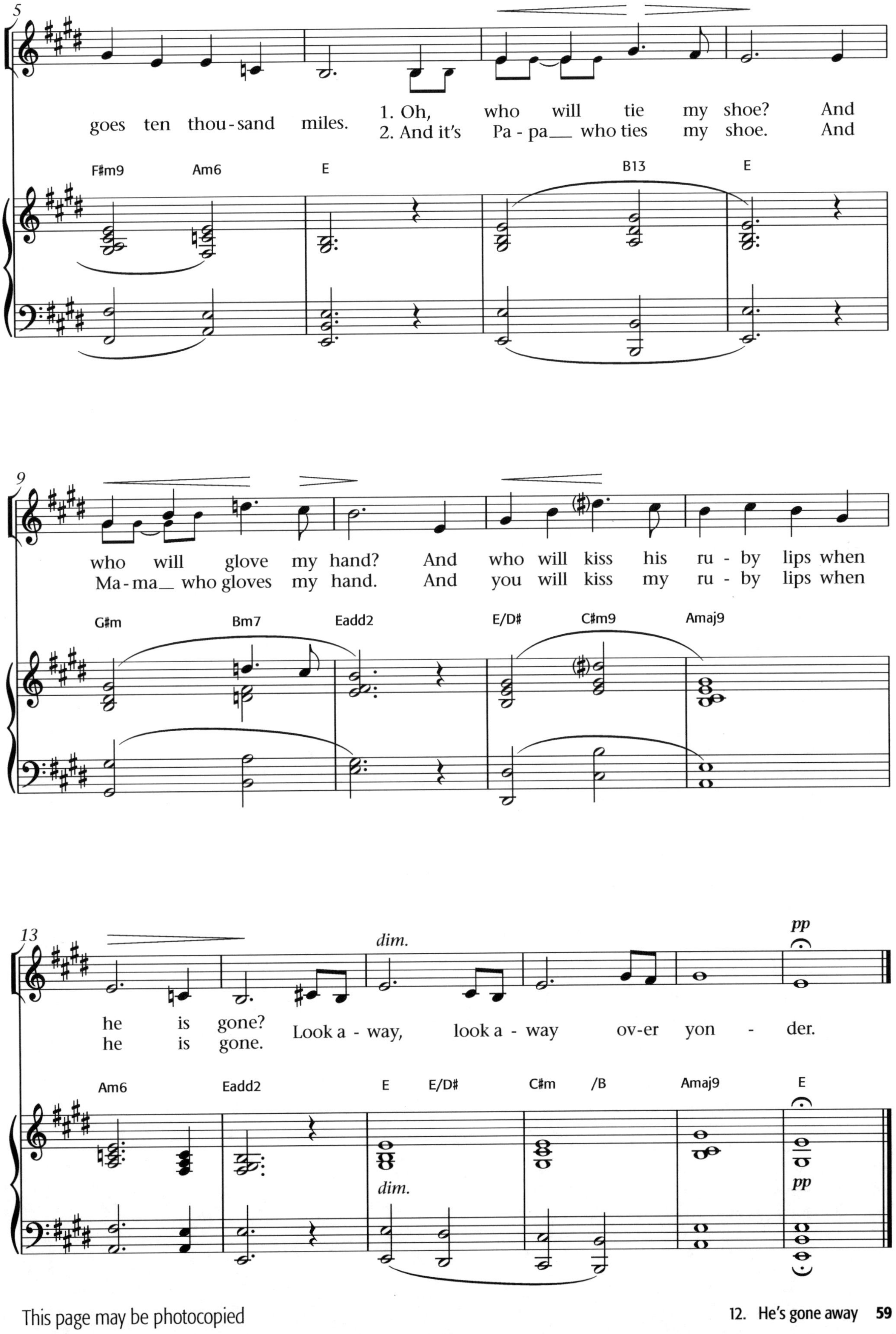
5
goes ten thou-sand miles.
1. Oh, who will tie my shoe? And
2. And it's Pa - pa__ who ties my shoe. And
F#m9 Am6 E B13 E
9
who will glove my hand? And who will kiss his ru - by lips when
Ma-ma__ who gloves my hand. And you will kiss my ru - by lips when
G#m Bm7 Eadd2 E/D# C#m9 Amaj9
13
dim.
pp
he is gone? Look a - way, look a - way ov-er yon - der.
he is gone.
Am6 Eadd2 E E/D# C#m /B Amaj9 E
dim.
pp

13 They'll Know We Are Christians By Our Love

RESOURCES ▶ SABar version: CD1 track 13 (performance); CD2 track 14 (backing)

▨ Information

Sacred music has evolved in many different ways over the past few centuries, and this folk favourite is no exception. Here we give it a funky, two-in-a-bar treatment. The pentatonic melody and limited range make this song easy to teach, fun to sing, and great for working on singing through the register changes in the voice. Two versions are provided: the first for unison voices, and the second a slightly extended arrangement for SABar.

▨ Starting

- Begin with some stretching and breathing exercises to gently warm up the voice (see pp. x–xii and 53); then allow 15–20 seconds of 'freestyle' stretching to free up the body and voice.
- Refer to the 'cry' and 'mix' sections on pp. 54–5 to prepare the voice for the sound you need.
- Sing the exercise below. Focus on tuning and aim for brightness on the 'cry' sound.

▨ Teaching and rehearsing

- Whichever version you choose, start with the melody. Stepping from side to side, teach this by rote, four bars at a time. Sit the words on the pulse. (Don't worry for now about bars 25–9 in the SABar version.)
- Now 'cry' through the melody a couple of times (the men may 'cry' up the octave, if possible). Slowly pull the 'cry' out of the voice, keeping the registers connected and the sound smooth. Maintain the resonance in the face (especially the men singing in middle and high registers). Refer to the exercises on pp. xiv and 55 whenever you come across register problems.
- As you move to higher pitches, maintain resonance and relaxation in your throat, chest, and face; keep the tone bright and energized.
- If you decide to do the SABar version, teach the parts in the same way as above. The second and third vocal parts are trickier but well worth the effort. Take your time.
- Now you've learnt the piece, try singing it with a slightly nasal tone and a fast vibrato; keep the sound bright and full. Listen to the CD demo or other gospel

groups such as the Richard Smallwood Singers for examples.
- Bars 25–9 in the SABar version contain a written-out break. You could also incorporate smears here, e.g. in bar 25 beat 3, arriving to the destination pitch around beat 3 of bar 26.

▨ Ideas

- Try clapping or clicking on beat 3 of each bar and incorporating the 'step-touch' movement introduced with No. 10 'This little light of mine'.
- This arrangement could alternatively be performed with guitar or unaccompanied.

▨ Listen out

- If there are tuning problems, identify the problem interval(s) and sing the pitches back and forth to get to know them better; then insert them back into the phrase.
- Check that the registers are smooth and connected; adding a little 'cry' to the voice will help.
- If using the piano accompaniment, keep the tempo steady and rock solid.
- Check that dynamics are in place in the SABar version.

▨ Performing

- Sing with resolve on your faces and in your posture.
- A unison beginning with harmony later could be very effective, as on the CD.
- If you're performing the SABar version, add more chest resonance (depth) to the sound—especially at the peak of the piece in bars 25–9—but keep the tone bright.

13 They'll Know We Are Christians By Our Love

Words: Peter Scholtes
Music: Carolyn Arends
arr. Steve Milloy

Unison version

Funky half-time march ♩ = 93

1. We are one in the Spi - rit, we are one in the Lord. We are one in the Spi - rit, we are one in the Lord. And we

2. We will walk with each other,
   we will walk hand in hand.
   We will walk with each other,
   we will walk hand in hand.
   And together we'll spread the news
   that God is in our land.

3. We will work with each other,
   we will work side by side.
   We will work with each other,
   we will work side by side.
   And we'll guard each one's dignity
   and save each one's pride.

4. All praise to the Father
   from whom all things come.
   And all praise to Christ Jesus
   his only Son.
   All praise to the Spirit
   who makes us all one.

© 1966 by FEL Church Publications Ltd. Assigned 1991 Lorenz Publishing Company

13 They'll Know We Are Christians By Our Love

SABar version

Words: Peter Scholtes
Music: Carolyn Arends, arr. Steve Milloy

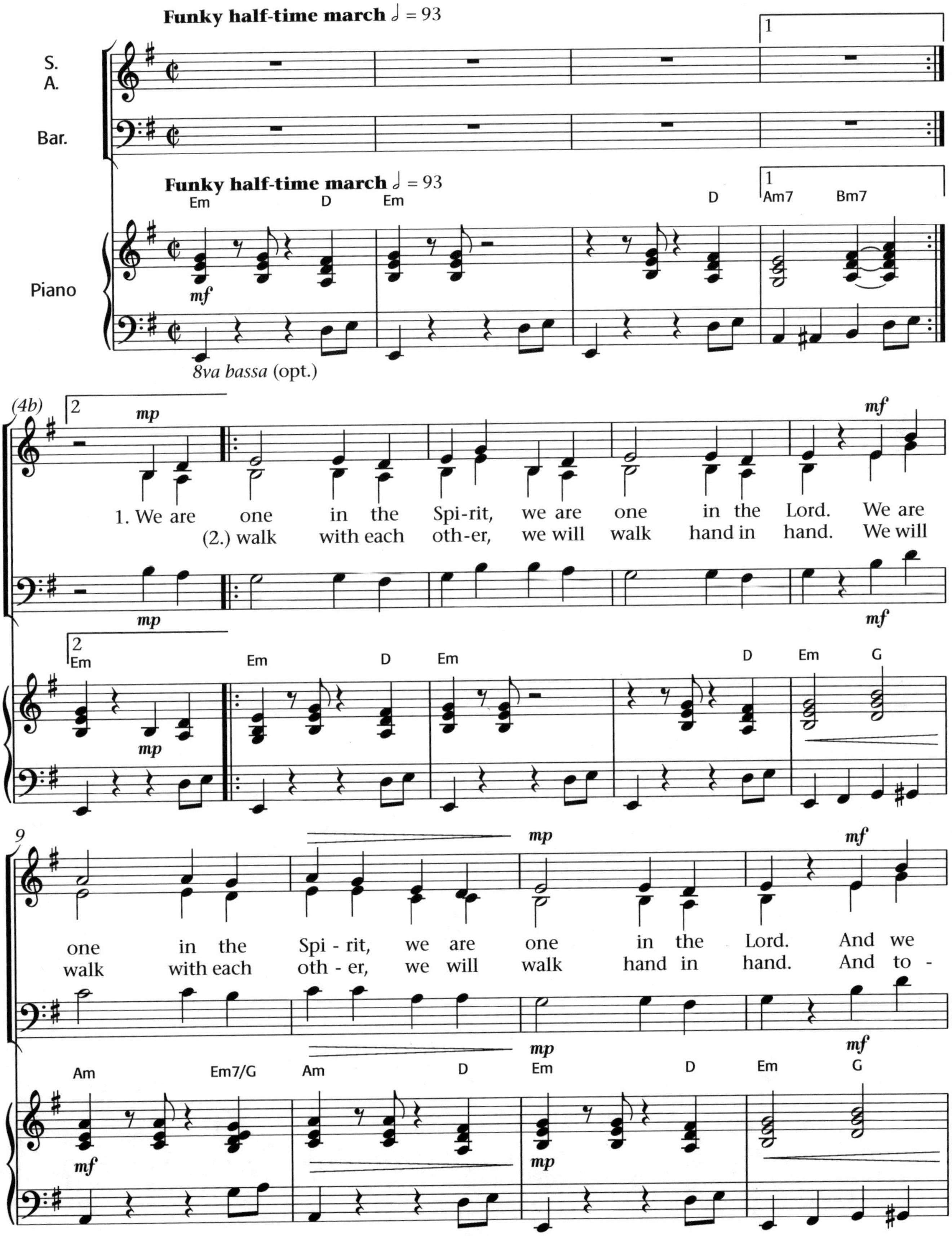

Funky half-time march 𝅗𝅥 = 93
S.
A.
Bar.
Piano
Em D Em D Am7 Bm7
mf
8va bassa (opt.)
(4b)
mp
1. We are one in the Spi-rit, we are one in the Lord. We are
(2.) walk with each oth-er, we will walk hand in hand. We will
Em Em D Em D Em G
9
one in the Spi - rit, we are one in the Lord. And we
walk with each oth - er, we will walk hand in hand. And to -
Am Em7/G Am D Em D Em G
mp
mf

Lyrics below the staves:

pray that all u-ni-ty may one day be re-stored. And they'll
-ge-ther we'll spread the news, that God is in our land.

know we are Christ-ians by our love, by our love. Yes, they'll

know we are Christ-ians by our love. 2. We will

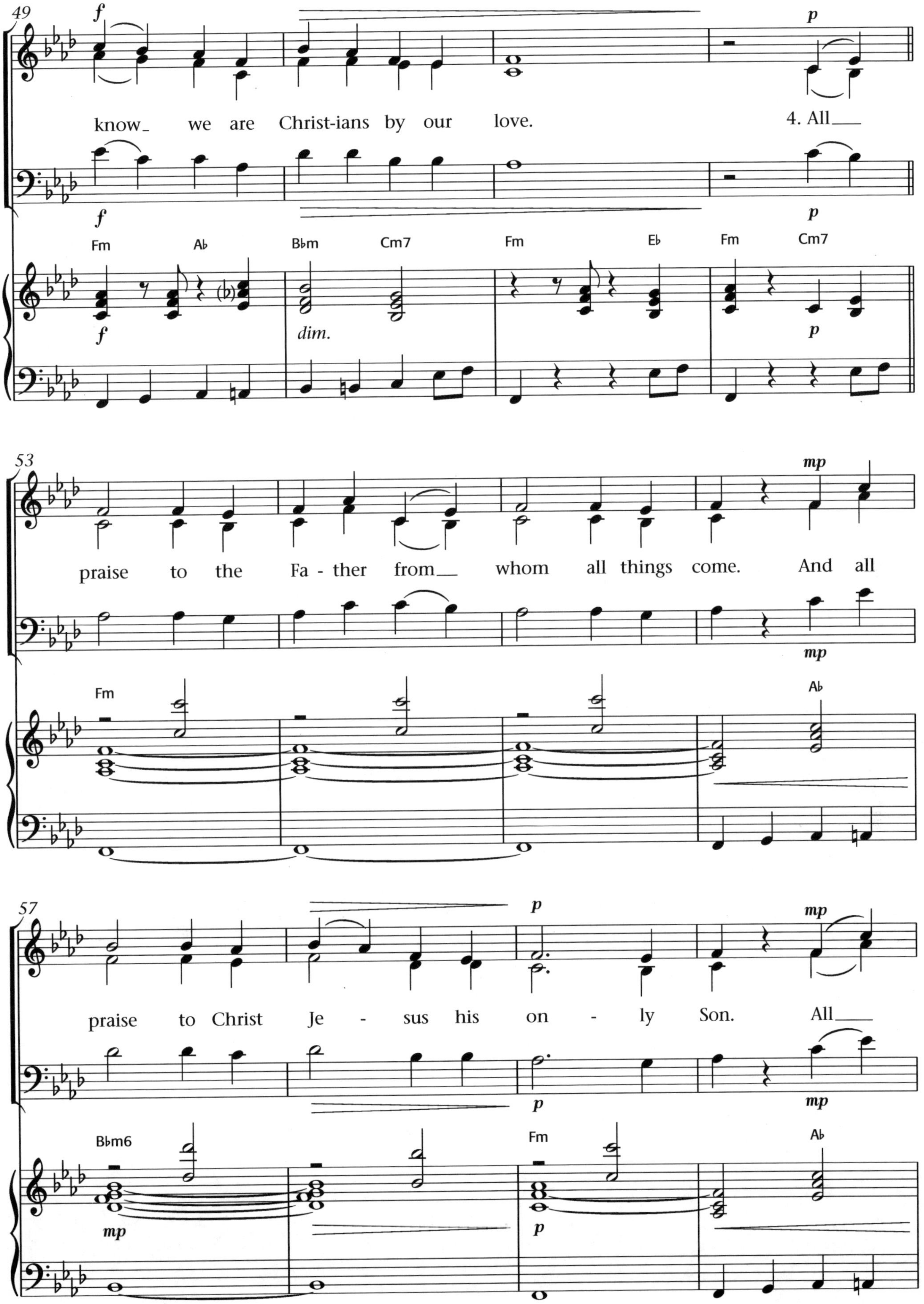

Lyrics under the music:

know we are Christ-ians by our love. 4. All

praise to the Fa-ther from whom all things come. And all

praise to Christ Je - sus his on - ly Son. All

61
p
mp
praise to the Spi - rit who makes us one. And they'll
Bbm6
Fm
Cm7
mp
p
65
rit.
know we are Christ-ians by our love, by our love. Yes, they'll
Dbmaj7
Db
Dbadd9
Eb
Fm
Ab
Bbm
Cm7
69
mf
slow, deliberate
know we are Christ-ians by our love.
Fm
Ab
Bbm
Cm7
Eb
Fsus
F
f

13 They'll Know We Are Christians By Our Love

Vocal score

Words: Peter Scholtes
Music: Carolyn Arends
arr. Steve Milloy

Funky half-time march ♩ = 93

S.
A.

(Piano introduction)

1. We are one in the Spi - rit, we are
(2.) walk with each oth - er, we will

Bar.

one in the Lord. We are one in the Spi - rit, we are one in the
walk hand in hand. We will walk with each oth - er, we will walk hand in

Lord. And we pray that all u - ni - ty may one day be re -
hand. And to - ge - ther we'll spread the news, that God is in our

- stored. And they'll know we are Christ-ians by our love, by our love. Yes, they'll
land.

Lyrics under the staves:

know we are Christ-ians by our love. 2. We will

Hey_____ ih yeah ih yeah ih yeah,___ uh huh.

3. We will work with each oth - er, we will

work side by side. We will work with each oth - er, we will work side by

side. And we'll guard each one's dig - ni - ty and save each one's pride. And they'll

This page may be photocopied

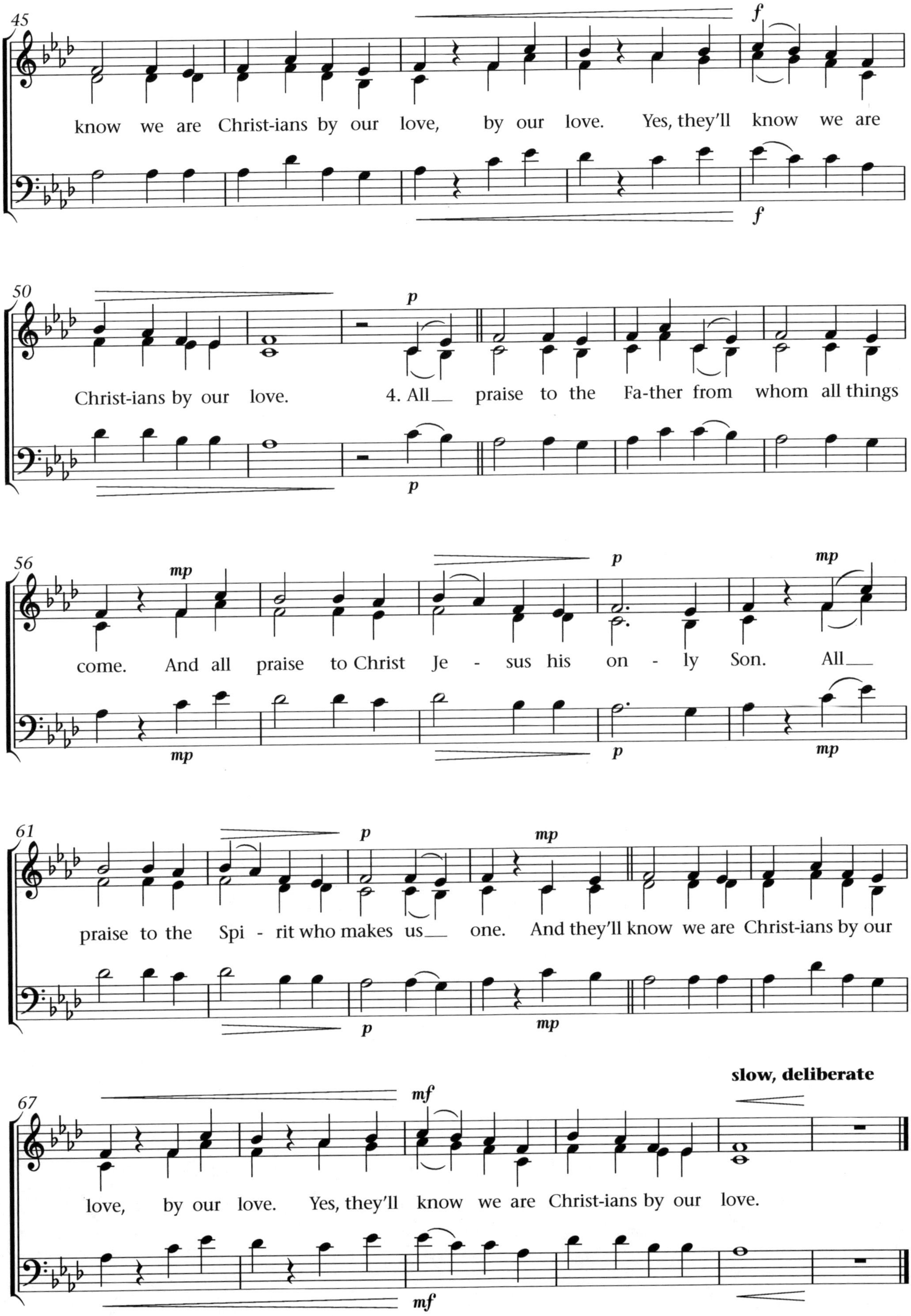

45
f
know we are Christ-ians by our love, by our love. Yes, they'll know we are
f
50
p
Christ-ians by our love. 4. All__ praise to the Fa-ther from whom all things
p
56
mp
p
mp
come. And all praise to Christ Je - sus his on - ly Son. All__
mp
p
mp
61
p
mp
praise to the Spi - rit who makes us__ one. And they'll know we are Christ-ians by our
p
mp
slow, deliberate
67
mf
love, by our love. Yes, they'll know we are Christ-ians by our love.
mf

14 I Want Your Love

RESOURCES ▶ CD1 track 14 (performance); CD2 track 15 (backing)

◻ Information

Whether it's from others or from ourselves, love is what we all need to get us through the day! This piece for upper voices is a light, funky original certain to get your singers moving!

◻ Starting

• Begin with the 'puppy dog' exercise (p. xiii) to work on creating a buzzing, even tone throughout the voice.
• Then, with a little 'cry' in the voice, sing the following. Keep the sound even and connected to the breath between register shifts—not too light on the higher notes, and not too heavy or dark on the lower notes. Then try it as a three-part round, with a part entering every two or four beats.

*uh*____
*ah*____

• Now sing the following in 'belt', or a mix of head and chest voice (see p. 55). Put a slight smear on beat 4 and keep the tone bright; depending on your group, you could also add a fast vibrato. Gradually extend the range upwards.

Hey, hey, hey, hey.____

• Finally, establish a tempo of about ♩ = 106 and sing the 'drum-kit' exercise below, to internalize the groove.

Doon doo dah_ k' doon_ doon dah k'

◻ Teaching and rehearsing

• This song could be taught by rote, perhaps with the verses written up on a board or projection. Here's how:
• With a 'cry' in the voice, teach the chorus (bars 19–26) to 'ah' or 'uh' before incorporating the lyrics. Add some accompaniment to keep the rhythm tight.
• Add the lower harmonies in bars 21 and 25.
• Still with a 'cry', teach bars 3–9 in the same way.

• Now move on to bars 27–34. Start by teaching Part 3, first to 'ah' or 'uh' and then with the lyrics; then add in Part 2, and finally Part 1. Hold the vowel in the word 'Love's' and place the ending consonants ('v's') at the beginning of the next word.
• Now in 'belt', sing bars 11–18 to 'ah' or 'ay' (no diphthong) and then add the words. Start with the top part and then teach the lower harmonies, before trying all three parts together; make sure all voices are moving as one.
• Pay attention to vowels that may need modification, e.g. in bars 27–34 the 'uh' sound in 'love' becomes 'ah' in 'belt'.
• Finally, put the whole song together. Try to create a contrast between the soft and lyrical 'I want your love' in bars 27–34 and the slightly edgier section at bars 11–18.

◻ Ideas

• This song can be sung with any accent, but it works particularly well with urban American 'street' pronunciation, as on the CD (i.e. 'don't want a' becomes 'dohn wanna', and 'can't' with an 'ah' becomes 'can't' rhyming with 'ant'). If you are changing your pronunciation, make sure the words can still be understood.
• Try using a soloist on one or both verses. Give them the freedom to stray from the written line.
• The score indicates a fall-off in bar 26. Feel free to add additional smears or fall-offs throughout (e.g. in bars 11 and 15), but be tasteful in your choices.
• To help your group with 'belt' and 'cry', listen to other singers of this genre like Chaka Khan, Natasha Bedingfield, or Rihanna.

◻ Listen out

• In bars 13 and 17, gauge your dynamic level so it balances out with the three-part section preceding it.
• Check that singers are placing the last syllable of 'Love's' carefully in bars 27–34.

◻ Performing

• Encourage your singers to be declamatory, and to enjoy the performance and have fun. This is not a song to be sung standing still!

14   I Want Your Love

Words: John Moysen,
with additional words by David Major
Music: Charles Beale and Steve Milloy

Medium funk; with honesty ♩ = 106

1. Don't want a
2. Don't want a

buc-ket full of dia - monds   or   of   gold.__
view of Cen-tral Park   or   gold-en   sands,__

Can't find no   hap-pi-ness in rich - es,   so I'm told.
and   I don't want to make my mark   in   for-eign lands.

10
div. (mf)
I don't want a sil-ver mine
I don't want the Gulf Stream
(3.) I don't want the life - style
Em7 Fmaj13 Dsus G7sus G7
(mf)
sim.
13
or a tricked out car.
or a sap-phire ring.
of the filth - y rich.
I don't
I don't
I don't
G7sus G7 G7sus
16
unis.
want an air - line. Can't use all that speed, there is just one thing I need.
have a big dream. Can't use all that greed, there is just one thing I need.
want the fake smile. Can't mix with that breed, there is just one thing I need.
G7 G7sus G7 B7+

This page may be photocopied

© Oxford University Press 2008

Chorus
19
f
I_ need your, I need your love t' get me through the day, babe.
Em7
Em7(♭5)
Bm7
Em7
f
last time to Coda
23
I_ want your, I want your love, now._
Em7(♭5)
Bm7
Em7
27
1
2
3
mp
Love's_ all I
Love's_ all I want. I_ want your_
Love's_ all I want. I_ want your love!_
Em7 Fmaj13 /B Em7 Fmaj13 /B Em7 Fmaj13 /B Em7 Fmaj13 /B
mf

This page may be photocopied

15 Silent night

RESOURCES ▶ CD1 track 15 (performance)

☐ Information

This is a contemporary jazz take on a Christmas classic. It is written for sopranos and altos but works equally well for mixed voices. Originally intended for a church context, it would create a meditative spot in a school Christmas concert. The pulse is free, and the piece as a whole should be taken very slowly, making a complete gesture of each phrase—almost like plainchant cocooned in the colour of the jazz chords.

☐ Starting

- Begin with some exercises on posture, then do some breathing exercises (see pp. x and xii).
- Inhale and say a short 'huh' gently, keeping the throat open. Feel the diaphragm working. Repeat, but this time say 'huh-haaah', supporting the long 'haaah'.
- Sing 'ah' on a mid-range note and then repeat the above exercise, to 'huh-haaah', on that pitch. Remember the feeling in your body. Now sing 'peace' on a rising 3rd of F and A, supporting the A and feeling your body work through the long note. Repeat on G and B, A and C♯, and finally B♭ and D.
- Get into pairs. As one person sings a pitch, the other should create a dissonance with it, a tone or semitone up or down. Feel the notes jangling against each other.

☐ Teaching and rehearsing

- If your group doesn't already know the melody, teach it to 'ah', phrase by phrase.
- Sing through the melody together to 'ah'. Use a slow tempo, so that every note and syllable is a separate musical gesture. Focus on getting a solid but quiet and relaxed tone, supporting long notes through to the end.
- Next, float the vowels and consonants on top of the melody, aiming to maintain the melodic flow and the openness of the 'ah' sound. Try singing the whole song using only vowels and omitting the consonants. (Note that the 'si-' of 'silent' and the 'ni-' of 'night' are diphthongs, containing essentially open 'ah' vowels with a short 'ee' at the end.)
- Now add in the lower harmony notes. Most are fairly easy to find, other than the final dissonance of each phrase. Teach the final 'heavenly peace' in two halves, noting the dissonance, but teaching the two lines separately—one ending on B♭ and the other on A.
- Practise the final fade on its own. All learn the 'peace' phrase and sing it initially in rhythmic unison and then so that each singer takes a decision about when to start and how long the word takes. Once this more varied

texture is in place, practise fading to nothing. Take 20 seconds initially, then perhaps a minute. Discuss what works best with your singers.

☐ Improvising toolbox

- Explore some common melodic shapes to be made out of a B♭ major scale. Divide the scale into two halves (B♭–F) and (F–B♭) and sing each stepwise. Then try a major pentatonic scale (B♭–C–D–F–G), and perhaps a scale in 3rds (B♭–D, C–E♭, D–F, etc.), or wider intervals like 6ths or 5ths. Play one of the piano chords in a static texture, and ask each person to sing one or possibly two long notes over the chord, and then move on to the next person. Each singer should explore a different shape.
- Next, play a game where each person makes up a short melodic shape of two to five notes, and repeats it; can everyone remember what they sang? Now allow the singer to change one note and use this strategy of repeating, or repeating with one note changed, as a way of creating a longer solo. Use this as the basis of some improvising in bars 15–18, where each phrase can be lengthened or shortened as you feel and even single notes can be expressive.

☐ Listen out

- The main technical danger-spot is the pitching of 'peace'. Make sure the vowel stays bright but open, and remind singers to support through to the end of the note.
- Ensure the beginning of each section is clearly marked. Listen for the re-entrance of the initial texture on B♭ after the solo passages.
- The harmony becomes tense and dissonant in bars 10–11, so the dynamics should naturally rise at that point and come back down at bars 12–14.

☐ Performing

- The performance should be mostly peaceful and move at a slow pace, exploring vocal dynamic range at the soft end.
- Consider adding extra instruments. A classroom composition on a 'starry night' theme using glockenspiels, recorders, keyboards, and percussion would work well as an introduction.
- The final fade can take as long as you need it to. Trust the singers to peter out on their own, and beware of over-directing the end.

For a free realization of the piano part visit www.oup.com/uk/music/voiceworks

15 Silent night

Franz Gruber
arr. Charles Beale

Without pulse – a meditation

e sim. – improvised sparkling, star-like, continuous texture, rippling up and down the voicing. Initially use given pitches in free order and rhythm, then embellish as necessary.

Si - lent night, Ho - ly night, All is calm,

all is bright; Round yon vir - gin mo - ther and child.

This page may be photocopied

Ho - ly In - fant so ten - der and mild, Sleep in hea - ven - ly

Cm13 Gm11 A7(♭9 13)

mf

last time **to Coda** ⊕

peace, Sleep___ in hea - ven - ly peace.

E♭7(♯11 ♭13) Cm11 E♭⁶₉ Gm11

mp *p*

℘ed.

SOLOS (vocal or instrumental) **D.C. al Coda** (on cue)

Gm11 E♭⁶₉ Cm11 E♭⁶₉

mp

⊕ **CODA** *pp*

gliss. *gliss.*

Peace___ peace___

All sing 'Peace' on these pitches round and round in own time as soloists.
Add other pitches and vocal sounds as necessary – 'sleep', 'ah', 'ssshhhh', etc.
Gradually fade to nothing. Piano stops first, then voices.

Gm11

pp

This page may be photocopied

16 Dancin' Till the Blues are Gone

RESOURCES ▶ CD1 track 16 (performance); CD2 track 16 (backing)

▣ Information

This is a 12-bar blues, revved up for the dance floor of the early 1960s!

▣ Starting

- Begin with some posture exercises (see p. x). Aim for a relaxed body as a solid basis of support on which to 'belt'.
- On a 'cry', then in 'belt', sing the following exercise—first to 'waa' and then to 'hey'. Sing it smoothly, maintaining a bright, slightly nasal tone and, if possible, a fast vibrato. Raise the starting note in half-step increments and add some piano if you can. Keep the sound open and relaxed at all times. You may feel that you need to make the tone thinner as you go higher to maintain your 'belt'. This is a good thing—you're 'belting' correctly!

- Divide the group into two. On a 'cry', then in 'belt', sing the following exercise, once again raising the starting note by step, to a B♭ in the top part. If necessary, minimize the vibrato to secure the tuning.

- Finally, establish a tempo of ♩ = 85. Click on beats 2 and 4, and then sing the hi-hat part below.

- Now try the drum part. Divide into two groups—one on each part—and gradually work the tempo up to ♩ = 168.

▣ Teaching and rehearsing

- First speak, then sing, the bridge and chorus (upbeat to bar 25 to end). In 'belt', upper voices (including men who decide to sing up the octave) may decide to modify vowels in bar 28 ('little Miss Lucy' modifies closer to 'lay-dahl mace luu-say').
- Do the same with the verses (bars 13–16). As before, the lower voices won't need to modify any vowels, but upper voices may want to modify 'can' (bar 14) and 'once for me' (bar 16), which become closer to 'cane' and 'wahns far mayee'. Let your ear be your guide regarding how much modifier to use, making sure your group is physically comfortable producing the tone.
- Next, speak and then sing the backing vocals; if possible, add a fast, shimmery vibrato on the long notes. Make sure the rhythm and tuning are precise and clean.
- Divide into two groups, with an equal number of male and female voices in each. Everyone should sing the verses (v. 1 female voices, v. 2 male voices) and bridge (everyone), then split into parts for the chorus. You might want to mix it up and have some lower voices sing the upper part at pitch and some upper voices sing the lower part at pitch. Use discretion, and don't overpower the lead line.

▣ Listen out

- Check tuning in the backing vocals. Minimize the vibrato and keep the half-step movements small.

▣ Ideas

- If the music moves you to dance, then dance! Even simple choreography can be fun and entertaining. Why not use staging to emphasize the difference between the 1st and 2nd verses?
- Try making up verses of your own. Personalize the song!
- To help your group get into the style, listen to other singers of this genre including Ray Charles, Tina Turner, the Coasters, the Ronettes, and Dee Dee Sharp—also mid-1960s British groups like the Beatles.

▣ Performing

- Encourage your group to be flexible in their delivery and to put their souls into the performance. Without compromising pitch and accuracy, this song should sound and feel like the music you hear on popular radio. Adding smears and fall-offs, and singing with soul, will help to convey this to the audience.
- This piece works well with a range of scorings and textures. Try using soloists, groups, or sections on the verses.

16 Dancin' Till the Blues are Gone

Fast 'twist'; party time! ♩ = 168

Steve Milloy

v. 1: upper voices
v. 2: lower voices

1. Hey there, boy, look-in' fine as can be,___
2. Hey, lit-tle la-dy with the fan-cy curl,___

let me see ya move it, groove it once for me.____
get out on the floor, won't you give me a whirl?_

Chorus
f
mel. only

Come on,____

gliss.

shake____ it like ya got no bone.____

backing vocals
mf

bop shu bop bah____ buh dah buh shu bop   bop shu bop bah

G7

D7

mf

We're gon-na dance babe, danc - in' till the blues are gone.

____ buh dah buh shu bop   bop shu bop   bop shu bop

A7

G7

This page may be photocopied

23
1
2
mp
We're gon-na
mp
bop shu bop shu bop
bop We're gon-na
D7
A7
A7
25
unis.
swim an' po-ny like Bo-ny Ma-ro-ne. Jerk, wa-tu-si, like
D
mp
28
Chorus
f
1
lit-tle Miss Lu-cy! Come on, shake it like ya got no bone.
2
mf
lit-tle Miss Lu-cy! bop shu bop bah buh dah buh shu bop
D7
G7
gliss.
f
mf

Lyrics:

We're gon-na dance, babe, danc-

bop shu bop bah___ buh dah buh shu bop bop shu bop

- in' till the blues are gone.

bop shu bop bop shu bop shu bop bop

This page may be photocopied

17 Straighten Up and Fly Right

RESOURCES ▶ CD1 track 17 (performance); CD2 track 17 (backing)

☐ Information

'Straighten Up and Fly Right' was written and introduced by Nat 'King' Cole, and the lyrics were inspired by a saying of his father's. This arrangement is for upper voices (or lower voices down the octave) and can be sung in one, two, or three parts. The song works well at almost any tempo, but, to sing like Cole, keep the delivery smooth, relaxed, and swinging—and don't rush.

☐ Starting

- Singing has been referred to as 'acting on prolonged pitches'. Work on the 'acting' part by encouraging singers to think of an experience they enjoyed and then to make the face that shows that feeling. Then ask some volunteers to shout out an emotion (afraid, angry, serious, dejected, ecstatic, etc.), and ask the rest of the group to make an appropriate face and hold it for five seconds.
- See the first two bullets of 'Starting' in the workshop for No. 1 'Swing Time' to review the concept of swing; now do the 'puppy dog' exercise on p. xiii.
- Sing the following exercise to establish the range of this piece and the scale tones used. The tone should be warm and inviting, with minimal vibrato. Raise the starting note in semitone steps, up to E.

☐ Teaching and rehearsing

- At a steady tempo, speak the lyrics section by section, making sure you maintain the swing. The stresses should be slight, but enough to give the music a forward motion.
- Next, sing the melody, keeping up the swing. The pronunciation should be clean but the delivery cool and relaxed. Don't worry at this stage about the delayed consonants in bars 8, 10, etc.
- Practise the delayed consonants by singing the 'Delay i - t' exercise on the next page. Note the kick in the pronunciation of the lyrics and the percussive element this adds to the singing. Make sure all notes are held for

their full value—they should have a stretched feeling—but also ensure that there is space between the delayed consonant and the preceding pitch.
- Now sing the song again with the delayed consonants in place. Try to make cut-offs 'upward' motions, especially on the delayed consonants. This helps to keep the sound forward-moving and the release energized.
- This piece may also be performed in unison or two parts (omitting the second Soprano part). Try introducing additional parts section by section, starting with the Alto then Soprano 2.

☐ Ideas

- Below the score is a scat chorus that could be inserted at bar 43 (after the 1st-time bar). You could use the piano backing and make up your own scat solos, or perform as written, omitting the sopranos the first time through. Go back to bar 27 after the scat section and use the second ending. (NB the CD backing does not accommodate the scat section.)
- Listen to the original Nat 'King' Cole Trio recording, as well as versions by Diana Krall, the Andrews Sisters, Marvin Gaye, and others. Find your favourites and compare styles.

☐ Listen out

- Check that the pitch is sustained on repeated notes and that melodic and harmonic intervals are accurate. Sing any problematic melodic intervals back and forth to get to know them better.

☐ Performing

- Make sure the humour of the lyrics shows in the faces of the singers. If they don't convey it, the audience will miss out on a vital aspect of the piece.

'Delay i-t' exercise

Medium Swing ♩ = 120

De - lay____ i - t, de - lay____ i - t.

On____ the right tra-ck, ta - kin' no sla-ck, jus' laid ba - ck.

17 Straighten Up and Fly Right

Nat 'King' Cole and Irving Mills
arr. Steve Milloy

Medium-fast swing ♩ = 132

3
buz - zard took a mon - key for a ride in the air. The
buz - zard took a mon - key for a ride in the air. The
A6
D6
D#°7
p
5
mon - key thought that ev - 'ry - thing was on the square. The
mon - key thought that ev - 'ry - thing was on the square. The
A/E
F9
E9
7
buz - zard tried to throw the mon - key off his ba - ck. The
buz - zard tried to throw the mon - key off his ba - ck. The
A
D6
D#°7

9
mon - key grabbed his neck and said 'Now list - en, Ja - ck!'
f
mon - key grabbed his neck and said 'Now list - en, Ja - ck!'
f
A/E
A6/9
f
11
mp
Straight-en up 'n' fly righ - t.
Straight-en up 'n' fly
mp
Straight-en up 'n' fly righ - t.
Straight-en up 'n' fly
A7/G D/F# Am7/E A7 D6 A/C#
p mp p
14
righ - t.
Straight-en up 'n' fly righ - t.
Cool
righ - t.
Straight-en up 'n' fly righ - t.
Cool
Bm7 E7sus E7+ A A7/G D/F# Am7/E A7
mp p mp

17
down, pa-pa, don't you blow your to - p. Ain't no use in div -
D6 A/C♯ Bm7 E7+ A A7/G
f mp p mf
20
- in'. What's the use of jiv - in'? Straight-en up 'n' fly
D/F♯ Am7/E A7 D6 A/C♯ Bm7 E7sus E7+ A A7/G
mp p
24
righ - t. Cool down, pa-pa, don't you blow your to - p.' The
D/F♯ Am7/E A7 D6 A/C♯ Bm7 E7 A6/9
f mf mp p

buz - zard told the mon - key, 'You are chok - in' me.__ Re -

buz - zard told the mon - key, 'You are chok - in' me.__ Re -

- lease your hold and I will set you free.'__ The

- lease your hold and I will set you free.'__ The

mon - key looked the buz - zard right dead in the eye and said, 'Your

mon - key looked the buz - zard right dead in the eye and said, 'Your

(opt. comic spoken solo)

33
sto - ry's so touch - in' but it sounds like a lie.'
sto - ry's so touch - in' but it sounds like a lie.'
E13
A6/9
f
35
mp
Straight-en up 'n' fly righ - t. Straight-en up 'n' stay
mp
Straight-en up 'n' fly righ - t. Straight-en up 'n' stay
A7/G D/F# Am7/E A7 D6 A/C#
p mp p
38
righ - t. Straight-en up 'n' fly righ - t. Cool
righ - t. Straight-en up 'n' fly righ - t. Cool
Bm7 E7sus E7+ A A7/G D/F# Am7/E A7
mp p mp

41
down, pa-pa, don't you blow your to - p.' The blow your top.'
down, pa-pa, don't you blow your to - p.' The blow your top.'
D6 A/C♯ Bm7 E7 A6/9 Bm7 E7 A F7
43
Straight-en up 'n' fly righ - t. Straight-en up 'n' do righ - t.
Straight-en up 'n' fly righ - t. Straight-en up 'n' do righ - t.
B♭ B♭7/A♭ E♭/G B♭m7/F B♭7 E♭6 B♭/D Cm7 F7sus F7+
47
Straight-en up 'n' fly righ - t. Cool down, pa-pa, don't you
Straight-en up 'n' fly righ - t. Cool down, pa-pa, don't you
B♭ B♭7/A♭ E♭/G B♭m7/F B♭7 E♭6 B♭/D

50

blow your top. Fly right!

blow your top. Fly right!

C9 F13 B♭maj7 /D E♭ G♭7/E F7sus B♭9

Optional scat chorus

42a

S.1
(S.2)

2nd time only

blow your to - p.' *Shop shah buh dah bah doo dah__ bup*

A.

blow your to - p.' *Shoo bee doo whee bop doo bop bad dahl you dah__ shah*

Bm7 E7 A$_9^6$ E9(#5) A A9/C# D D#°7

Piano

bop shah bah dah bah doo wah___ dah bah dah bah dah dot bah

whee bop doo bah doo bah___ bah doo bah___ shop shah eeyoo dot bah

A/E F#7(b9) Bm E7 A A9/C#

bah dah bah dah bah

dah yule dah___ shah dah bah doo whee_ 'n doo bah.___ bah shah bah doo

D D#°7 A/E F#7(b9) Bm7 E13

(sing)

(back to bar 27)

dah bah doo wah___ doo dot!

The

dah bah doo wah___ doo dot!

The

B7/D# E13 A7

This page may be photocopied

17 Straighten Up and Fly Right

Vocal score

Nat 'King' Cole and Irving Mills
arr. Steve Milloy

Medium-fast swing ♩ = 132

S.1 (S.2)
A buz-zard took a mon-key for a

A.
A buz-zard took a mon-key for a

ride in the air. The mon - key thought that ev - 'ry - thing was

ride in the air. The mon - key thought that ev - 'ry - thing was

on the square. The buz - zard tried to throw the mon - key

on the square. The buz - zard tried to throw the mon - key

off his ba - ck. The mon-key grabbed his neck and said 'Now list-en, Ja - ck!'

off his ba - ck. The mon-key grabbed his neck and said 'Now list-en, Ja - ck!'

Straight-en up 'n' fly____ righ - t. Straight-en up 'n' fly_

_ righ - t. Straight-en up 'n' fly___ righ - t. Cool

_ down, pa - pa, don't you blow your to - p. Ain't no use in div -

- in'. What's the use of jiv - in'? Straight-en up 'n' fly_

_ righ - t. Cool_ down, pa - pa, don't you blow your to - p.' The

This page may be photocopied

Measure 27:
buz - zard told the mon - key, 'You are chok - in' me.___ Re -

buz - zard told the mon - key, 'You are chok - in' me.___ Re -

Measure 29:
- lease your hold and I will set you free.'___ The

- lease your hold and I will set you free.'___ The

Measure 31:
cresc.

(opt. comic spoken solo)

mon - key looked the buz - zard right dead in the eye and said, 'Your

cresc.

mon - key looked the buz - zard right dead in the eye and said, 'Your

Measure 33:
sto - ry's so touch - in' but it sounds like a lie.'

sto - ry's so touch - in' but it sounds like a lie.'

Measure 35:
mp

Straight-en up 'n' fly____ righ - t. Straight-en up 'n' stay_

mp

Straight-en up 'n' fly____ righ - t. Straight-en up 'n' stay_

38

_ righ - t. Straight-en up 'n' fly____ righ - t. Cool

_ righ - t. Straight-en up 'n' fly____ righ - t. Cool

41

f *mf* *f*

_ down, pa-pa, don't you blow your to - p.' The blow your top.'

f *mf* *f*

_ down, pa-pa, don't you blow your to - p.' The blow your top.'

43

mf

Straight-en up 'n' fly____ righ - t. Straight-en up 'n' do____ righ - t.

mf

Straight-en up 'n' fly____ righ - t. Straight-en up 'n' do____ righ - t.

47

Straight-en up 'n' fly____ righ - t. Cool____ down, pa-pa, don't you

Straight-en up 'n' fly____ righ - t. Cool____ down, pa-pa, don't you

50

f *ff*

blow your top. Fly right!

f *ff*

blow your top. Fly right!

This page may be photocopied

18 Sweet Tea

RESOURCES ▶ CD1 track 18 (performance); CD2 track 18 (backing)

Information

This is a slow swing ballad in the style of the famous 1950s *Sing a Song of Basie* album by Lambert, Hendricks, and Ross, where the voices imitate the sound of a big band. More recent vocal groups that phrase in a similar way include the Hi-Lo's, Double Six, the Swingle Singers, Take 6, and The Real Group.

Starting

• Get the slow swing started by tapping (or saying 'do' to) a steady 4/4 pulse at ♩ = 75. Repeat 'do-ba do-ba do-ba do-ba' round and round, placing the 'ba' in a relaxed triplet with a little extra weight. Clap or tap on beats 2 and 4 as well, to feel the backbeat.

• Next, sing up and down a major pentatonic scale, with the same feel:

• Practise saying some of the key rhythms of the tune in time with the pulse, choosing suitable syllables for long and short notes. For example, say the first phrase (bar 3) to 'do-bup', making the 'do' longer with a slight crescendo and the 'bup' short and hard.

• Next, try the phrase in bar 9, again adding weight to the offbeat. Take care not to rush.

Teaching and rehearsing

• Make sure the group is standing close together, so they can hear one another clearly.

• This arrangement is essentially in two parts, with optional four-part moments. Phrasing and ensemble is all-important, so begin by teaching small sections of the melody in unison, phrase by phrase. It can often be easier to work by ear to begin with, using the notation as a reminder once the phrasing and rhythm are internalized.

• Next, teach the lower parts (these could be sung by women/girls too, if sufficiently experienced), assigning the optional smaller notes to a four-part SATB texture as appropriate for your group.

Ideas

• You could insert a repeat back to bar 2 at the end of bar 33, including the piano part in bar 2. Try adding a vocal or instrumental solo in the first half of the repeat, with the choir coming back in on the bridge (bar 19).

Listen out

• Listen to the end of each phrase and make sure everyone comes off together.

• The need for rhythmic incisiveness and the feeling of swing can result in over-singing. Aim for a quiet, intimate sound (see 'Performing', below), adding in the rise and fall to achieve a blended group sound.

• Choose a relatively straightforward unison passage and listen for blend. Is anyone sticking out above the group sound? Adjust the balance so that the sound is seamless, blended, and rich. Try a group crescendo and diminuendo. Did everyone go up and down together?

• If you are based outside the US think about vowels in this American style. It can be good to Americanize the words to some extent as this will often brighten the sound overall, but take care to keep the sound rounded and not too harsh.

Performing

• To perform with real authenticity, singers should be grouped around a set of microphones on stands and, if possible, have one mike each. This will necessitate a brief sound-check to get an appropriate balance between voices. If available, add bass and drums too.

• Would a small amount of movement help to communicate the tune? Sometimes moving together can help the groove settle, as everyone externalizes the pulse. But keep it natural and relaxed so it doesn't distract the audience from your sound.

18 Sweet Tea

Words: John Moysen
Music: Charles Beale

Swing; with sincerity ♩ = 75

Lyrics:
Each day, as I a-rise, that six o'-clock a-larm bell I_ des-pise;_ you're up, fix-in' my drink, sweet tea helps me op-en my eyes.

10
I stir, so do you
D7+ Gm7 G#o Am7 D7+
13
while you pre-pare my fav-'rite mor - nin' brew. Oh! Love - ly,
G7 C9sus Am7 E♭maj7 D7(#9) G7 G#o
16
sweet and hot, my sweet tea helps me ban-ish the blues.
Am7 D7+ G7 C9sus C7 F6 F9/A

19
mf
Thank you, honey, that cup tastes so fine.
Well, thank you, honey, that cup tastes so fine,
Bb G7/B B° F6/C F9/A Bb G7/B B°
22
When you bring it up to me, I
tastes so fine. You bring it up
F/C F B9+ Bb6 B° F/C D9
25
know the sun is gon-na shine! My sky may be grey, but
know the sun is gon-na shine!
p
G9 C13(b9) D7+ Gm7 G#° Am7 D7+

Lyrics under the staves:

m. 29: one sip of that tea can get me fee-lin' O K. My su - gar

Chord symbols (m. 29–31): G7 C9sus Am7 E♭maj7 D7 D7(♯9) G7 G♯°

m. 32: lifts me so, my sweet tea helps me face a new day. Sweet tea,__ sweet tea,__

Chord symbols (m. 32–34): Am7 D7+ G13 C9sus C7 F6 F7+ B♭9

m. 35: sweet tea,__ sweet tea,__

So good__ for me____ It's plain to see__

Chord symbols (m. 35–37): B° F6/C F7+ B♭9 B° F6/C

This page may be photocopied

19 Song Without Words

RESOURCES   ▶ CD1 track 19 (performance); CD2 track 19 (backing)

Information

This gentle piece was written for a jazz workshop with boys and girls with experience in Anglican church music, and it works well in more resonant acoustics. The lower part is for altos, tenors, and those with changing voices, and has a more restricted range; while the optional descant contains a high G♯ (which can be omitted), to allow the sopranos to blossom. The melody and counter-melody contain a few tricky chromatic shifts, which make this piece less suitable for inexperienced singers; however, most can perform the backings and possibly the main melody, if taught by ear.

Starting

- Stretch up, to raise the rib-cage and open up the back. With both arms stretching upwards, lean back slightly and breathe in, then lean forward slightly and breathe out.
- Breathe all the way out. Hold, and feel the pressure to breathe in. On cue (a clap, perhaps), let the air fall back into the lungs in an involuntary inhale.
- Breathe in for four beats, then hold for four; breathe out for four beats, then rest for four. Repeat. Do the same for five beats, and work up to eight gradually.
- Next, work on the 'ah' vowel. First, all sing 'ah' on an F♯. Then sing up and down a Dorian mode—perhaps try F♯ Dorian, the scale of the improvised section in this piece:

- Yawn, and feel the space it creates at the back of the throat. Sing the same scale to 'oh'. Sing it to 'ah' again, this time with a hint of 'oh' to make the sound rounded and slightly darker. Try the different 'ah' sounds; agree which is right for your group here and blend.

Teaching and rehearsing

- Teach the melodic shapes that repeat, starting with this one in its two different pitches:

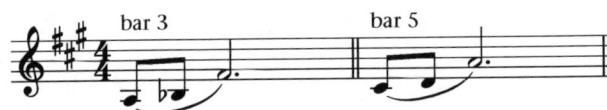

Then add the link between these bars and sing the phrase complete.

- Teach the following phrases in the same way, starting with the repeating shapes and then joining them together:

- Then sing the melody complete. Teach the counter-melody in the same way, before trying both parts together.
- Now add in the optional descant, if your group is performing it. A small but pure sound will work fine here. When singing high, remind singers not to open their mouths too wide.

Improvising toolbox

This song needs a solo section for the form to work properly. An improvising instrumental soloist could play the solo while the vocal group sings the backings. This song is particularly useful for beginner vocal improvisers. For suggestions of melodic ideas, listen to the CD demo or try the following:

Starting from the pulse:
- Have the group sing a confident 'ah' on an F♯.
- Still on F♯, sing to 'la' a steady stream of crotchets/quarter-notes and then quavers/eighth-notes. Repeat, but this time encourage the singers to add some longer notes and gaps wherever each singer feels like it—still on only one note. The result should be a cacophony of 'la's, with every individual singing a different rhythm.
- Now do the same, but this time allow them to sing F♯ and one extra note of their choice.
- Finally, allow a wider range of pitch, but ensure the focus is still on rhythmic interest.

Starting from the scale:
- Ask the group to sing up and down the first five notes of the Dorian scale (see 'Starting', above). Then ask them to choose one pitch and sing it—you will get a random chord or cluster, depending on the number in your group. Suggest that they cannot sing the same note as their neighbour. Repeat, with each singer using a different note.
- Now play an improvising game. Do not insist on the Dorian mode now, though many of the pitches will come from that. Initially, one volunteer steps forward and sings to 'la' a single long note over the solo groove, i.e. not a melody. They can choose any note they like,

and sing it confidently for as long as they want to. After a pause for a breath, they should then sing a second note—and so on. If there is a group, they should stand in a circle and each sing a single note, one after the other.

- Next, each person sings two notes—as 'la' [pause] 'la'. They can be the same as each other, or the second may be higher or lower. Repeat and/or go around the room giving everyone the chance to sing two notes. Perhaps repeat with three.
- In the following session, you could repeat this game (using two notes) as a warm up. Once this is in place, allow your singers to sing as many notes as they like—i.e. to carry on. Make sure they give a clear signal (perhaps a nod) to show that they have stopped and the next person is to continue.
- Choose the best ones for the performance, solo or in combination; if you like, allow a section after the solos where everyone gets to improvise single long notes together before the melody comes back. The result can be very expressive and should begin to rise and fall interestingly after a while as the group members begin to listen to each other more.

▢ Listen out

- Tone on the first entry is likely to be quieter and darker because of the low pitch. If it is too quiet, add a few altos to the melody group if necessary, to create a richer, fuller sound.
- Check that the breath is sustained through the long notes so they have energy to the end.
- Watch cut-offs after long notes. If necessary, train each group to come off together without the leader cuing them, by looking at each other and stopping the sound together.

▢ Performing

- Begin with the melody alone, then add the counter-melody. Either could be taken by a soloist if you have one, or by the main group.
- The solo section needs to go around at least twice.
- On cue or on the second time, add in one or two backings, depending on the size and vocal range of your group. Use the backings to build the dynamic gradually.
- Open the song out into a final louder statement of the melody on the *da capo*. This can also include the descant.
- Finish with the coda, which should diminish gradually in energy and become increasingly calm. Embellish this with a number of soloists doing question and answer on long 'ah' sounds or some final instrumental soloing. End on cue when it feels right, but don't be afraid to go round one more time if a solo is suddenly going well.

19 Song Without Words

Gently flowing; straight 8s ♩ = 105

Charles Beale

This page may be photocopied

16
ah
ah
ah
ah
F#m9
Dmaj9
C#7+
SOLO (voice or instrument)
19
F#m9
on cue backing 2
div.
mf
ba dup ba ba dup
ba dup ba ba dup
on cue backing 1
mf
ah
ah
F#m9
mf (optionally embellish)

ba___ dup ba ba dup

ba___ da da da da dup

ah___

ah___

Dmaj9

ba___ dup ba ba dup

ba___ dup ba ba dup

ah___

ah___

Dmaj9

This page may be photocopied

This page may be photocopied

19. **Song Without Words** **111**

20 Don't Let the Door Hitcha

RESOURCES ▶ CD1 track 20 (performance); CD2 track 20 (backing)

■ Information

This is one of three songs in this collection for girls' or women's voices. The style is similar to Chaka Khan or Beyoncé, and the lyrics are about inner strength and moving on, in the tradition of Gloria Gaynor's 'I Will Survive' or 'Survivor' by Destiny's Child. The vocal parts are scored for SSA, and a simple piano accompaniment has been provided; this is a great number in which to add guitar and drums.

■ Starting

- Do some simple stretching and breathing exercises to get the body moving and the breathing apparatus up and running.
- Begin with the 'leaping up smoothly' and 'range extension' exercises on p. xiv to work on a buzzing, even tone throughout the voice.
- For good diction and loose, relaxed lips, try the 'popacatapetal' exercise on p. xv.
- In 'belt', sing the following in a declamatory style. Start with the top line, then add the parts one by one. Try to make it soulful—use a bright tone and a fast, wide vibrato. Start the smeared notes softly and grow as you approach the written pitch.

When this is confident, work upwards step by step. Reinforce the first chord of each two-bar phrase on the piano.

- Divide into three groups and perform the exercise below, to internalize the groove. One group stomps and claps; one clicks; and one claps:

When this is secure, learn the chorus lyrics (bars 23–30) and try chanting them in rhythm over the backing.

■ Teaching and rehearsing

- Now learn the chorus melody, shown in Parts 2 and 3. Keep the rhythm tight and aim for relaxed lips and a bright, effortless, soulful sound.
- When this is confident, all learn the descant shown in Part 1. Try using modifiers at full strength. Say, and then sing, 'Dahn't late thah dahr hate yah yay-ay-yay'; use more modifiers in the higher range than when the melody goes below a G. When everyone has learnt the descant, divide the group into two and sing both parts together.
- Now teach the verses in three sections: bars 3–9; 11–17; and 19–22. Start by all learning each part:
- Speak bars 3–9 in rhythm and then sing them, checking which notes need to be modified; add some accompaniment to provide a secure beat. Now learn bars 11–17 in the same way.
- Watch the rhythm in bars 12–13 and 16–17—the grace notes should be a quick smear. As is usual for pop melismas (single syllables set to more than one note), slightly stress the first note in each of these phrases. Check bar 15 for 'belt' modification.
- Next, teach and then add the backing parts. Keep them soft and smooth—there's no need to 'belt' until the pick-up to bar 18.
- Teach bar 18 with a bright, 'belting' tone quality and then learn bars 19–22. Check bars 18 and 22 (with pick-up) for modification. Now allocate voices to each part and reinforce learning by singing the whole song up to bar 30, with accompaniment.
- Finally, teach bars 31–8. Part 1 will need modification throughout this passage, as will Part 2 in bars 37–8. Start the smear in bar 38 softly and grow in dynamic as you approach the written pitch. Continue this crescendo to the bar-line, maybe even baring some teeth near the end for brightness!

■ Improvising toolbox

- Instead of the written-out descant in the chorus (Part 1), a soloist could create their own riffs. Try different things and see what your group likes.
- Bars 39–42 include an optional spoken solo. Encourage your singers to make up their own words, using words or phrases from the song or adding new ideas of their own. Share ideas and build confidence by asking for volunteers to read their thoughts to the group.

- Now add the piano backing and consider what style might be appropriate for each solo. This could be anything from a quiet rap seething with anger to a matter-of-fact spoken monologue. See what your singers come up with!
- If you decide to act out the solo, you could play the passage four times through, instead of twice as scored (and as on the CD backing).

Listen out

- Make sure the melismas or runs in Part 1 are clean and that each note is delineated. You don't have to add an 'h' to each note to do this; just don't smear them. Check bar 15.
- The backing vocals in bars 11–17 should not overpower the lead.

- Keep the sound vital and energized, and check that your group isn't over-singing. Most singers of this style of music know exactly what their voices can do, and even though they may stretch them to the limit, they never go beyond that point. They have to be able to sing tomorrow, and so do you!

Performing

- If you are adding the optional solo, decide who will perform this.
- Sometimes minimal staging is best: strong positions and movements will make the piece come alive and really convey the message to your audience. A good example of this is the Act 1 Finale in *Les Miserables*.

20 Don't Let the Door Hitcha

Words: John Moysen
Music: Steve Milloy

Latin House; with attitude! ♩ = 120

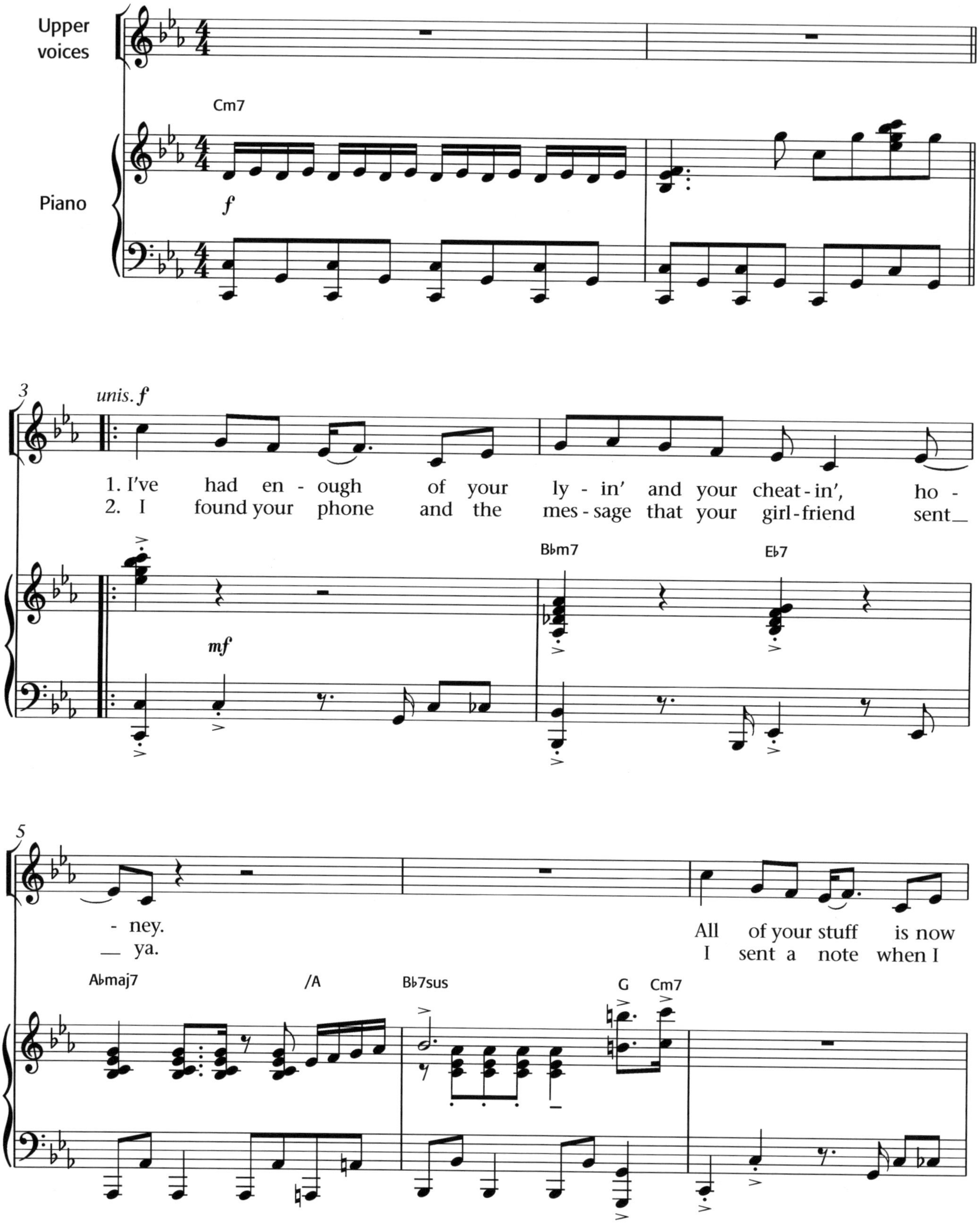

Upper voices
Piano
Cm7
f
3
unis. f
1. I've had en - ough of your ly - in' and your cheat - in', ho -
2. I found your phone and the mes - sage that your girl - friend sent
mf
B♭m7
E♭7
5
- ney.
ya.
All of your stuff is now
I sent a note when I
A♭maj7
/A
B♭7sus
G
Cm7

packed and wait-in' in your car.___
saw just what she had to say.___

You think that's rough? Just be glad that I don't want your mo-
I hope she's home when you go 'round with the things I left___

oh

ho___

- ney.___
- ya.___

ah

ha___

oh

ho___

I can be tough, so just
May-be she'll moan and like

Measure 16 (vocal lines):
hope that I don't go too far,_____ oh,_____ no! Some-thin'
me she'll send you on your way,_____ oh,_____ yeah! First I

(lower vocal) ah / oh,_____ no! Some-thin' / oh,_____ yeah! First I

Chords m.16: Gm7   Cm   A♭maj7   Gm7 Cm7   gliss.

Measure 19:
unis.
hap-pened o - ver-night, and I'm not a-bout to fight. You can
thought it was_ a phase, I've been liv-in' in_ a daze. Now I've

Chords m.19: Bm7   B♭m7   E♭7   E♭7sus

Measure 21:
1.,2.
walk right out that door, you don't live here a - ny-more.
3.
wok - en up to see_ that you're not the one for me!

Chords m.21: A♭maj7   Gm7 Fm7 Gm7 A♭maj7   B♭7sus

Chorus
opt. DESCANT
MELODY
unis.
Don't let the door hit-cha yeah - ee-eh!
Don't let the door hit-cha, don't let the door hit-cha,
Cm7
Bbm7
Eb7
Eb7sus
No, on your way out!
don't let the door hit - cha on your way out!
Abmaj7
Gm7
Fm7
Gm7
Abmaj7
Bb7sus
I'm old - er and wis - er, yeah - ee-eh!
I think she'll des - pise ya, yeah - ee-eh!
I'm old - er and wis - er, and ba - by I'm rich - er,
I think she'll des - pise ya, I bet ya she'll ditch ya,
Cm7
Bbm7
Eb7
Eb7sus

29
f
f
f
No, on your way out!
don't let the door hit - cha on your way out!
A♭maj7
Gm7
Fm7
Gm7
A♭maj7
B♭7sus
31
Look how far I fell for ten years of your lies.
A♭maj7
Gm7
34
1.,2.
3.
Don - 'cha ring my bell, I re -
Fm7

- fuse   to   com - pro - mise!

- fuse   to   com - pro - mise!

Bb7sus

G   Cm7

opt. spoken solo

1

(You know what? I gave you everything I had and I got nothing in return, so I've been doing a little thinkin'.

Cm7   Bbm7   Eb7   Abmaj7   Gm7

mp

42a

2

(end spoken solo)

Your bags are packed, the cab has been called, you've got to go. Thanks for playin'. Bye-bye.

Fm7 Gm7 Abmaj7 Bb7sus   Abmaj7   Gm7   Fm7   Gm7   Abmaj7   Bb7sus

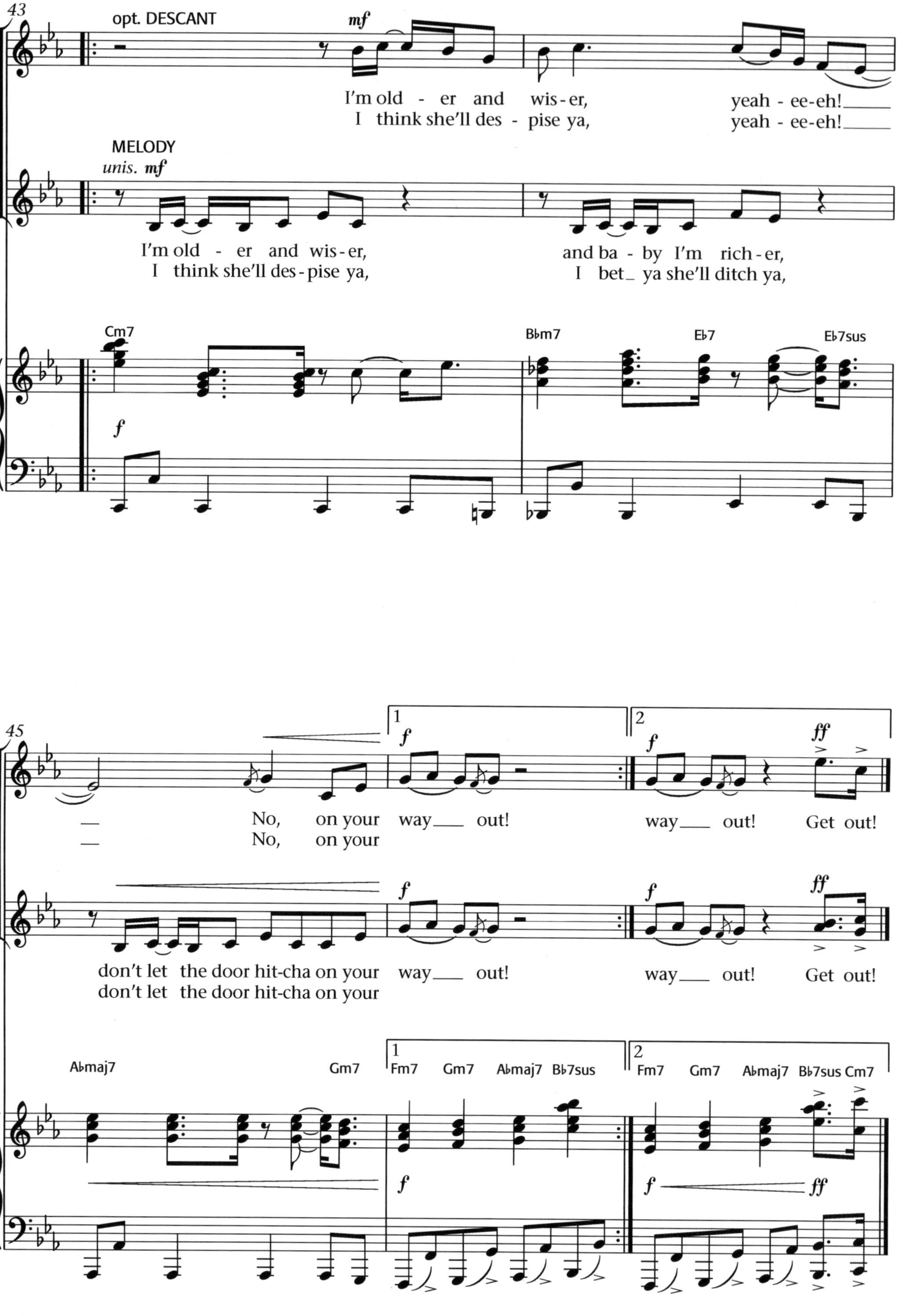

Lyrics under the music:

opt. DESCANT (voice 1):
I'm old - er and wis - er,   yeah - ee-eh!____
I think she'll des - pise ya,   yeah - ee-eh!____

MELODY unis. (voices 2/3):
I'm old - er and wis-er,   and ba - by I'm rich - er,
I think she'll des - pise ya,   I bet_ ya she'll ditch ya,

No,   on your way____ out!   way____ out!   Get out!
No,   on your

don't let the door hit-cha on your way____ out!   way____ out!   Get out!
don't let the door hit-cha on your

20 Don't Let the Door Hitcha

Vocal score

Words: John Moysen
Music: Steve Milloy

Latin House; with attitude! ♩ = 120

(Piano introduction)

Upper voices

unis. **f**

1. I've had en-ough of your ly-in' and your cheat-in', ho-
2. I found your phone and the mes-sage that your girl-friend sent

- ney.
- ya.

All of your stuff is now
I sent a note when I

packed and wait-in' in your car.
saw just what she had to say.

mf

You think that's rough? Just be glad that I don't want your mo - ney.
I hope she's home when you go 'round with the things I left ya.

mp

oh   ho   ah   ha

I can be tough, so just hope that I don't go too far,
May-be she'll moan and like me she'll send you on your way,

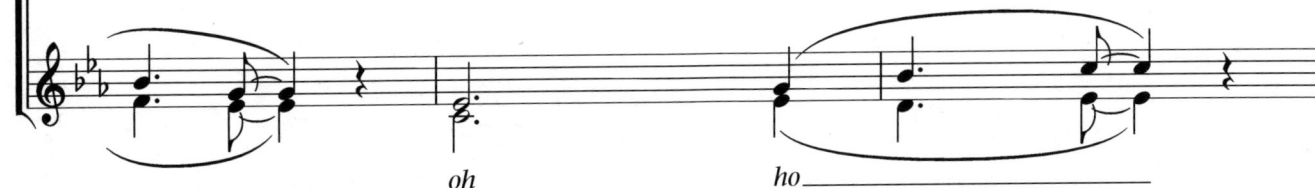

oh   ho

oh,_____ no! Somethin'
oh,_____ yeah! First I

ah
oh,_____ no! Somethin'
oh,_____ yeah! First I

hap-pened o - ver - night, and I'm not a - bout to fight. You can
thought it was_ a phase, I've been liv - in' in_ a daze. Now I've

walk right out that door, you don't live here a - ny - more.
wok - en up to see_ that you're not the one for me!

Chorus

opt. DESCANT

Don't let_ the door hit-cha yeah - ee - eh!_____

MELODY

Don't let_ the door hit-cha, don't let_ the door hit-cha,

This page may be photocopied

Lyrics under the music:

m. 25
No, on your way_____ out!
don't let_____ the door hit-cha on your way_____ out!

m. 27
I'm old - er and wis - er, yeah - ee - eh!_____
I think she'll des - pise ya, yeah - ee - eh!_____

I'm old - er and wis - er, and ba - by I'm rich - er,
I think she'll des-pise ya, I bet_ ya she'll ditch ya,

m. 29
No, on your way_____ out!
don't let_____ the door hit - cha on your way_____ out!

m. 31
Look how far_____ I fell_____ for ten years of_____ your lies._____

m. 34
Don - 'cha ring_____ my bell,_____
1.,2.
3.
I re -

(You know what? I gave you everything I had and I got nothing in return, so I've been doing a little thinkin'. Your bags are packed, the cab has been called, you've got to go. Thanks for playin'. Bye-bye.)

opt. DESCANT

I'm old - er and wis-er,
I think she'll des-pise ya,

yeah - ee-eh!
yeah - ee-eh!

MELODY

I'm old - er and wis-er,
I think she'll des-pise ya,

and ba - by I'm rich-er,
I bet ya she'll ditch ya,

No, on your way out! way out! Get out!
No, on your

don't let the door hit-cha on your way out! way out! Get out!
don't let the door hit-cha on your

This page may be photocopied

21 I'm Not Your Pet

RESOURCES ▶ CD1 track 21 (performance)

Information

This is a comic song in a 1950s doo-wop style, scored for a solo lead, backing vocals, and bass. The performance should be smooth, slick, and tongue-in-cheek, just like the style it's paying tribute to. This is a great song for male-voice choirs, from four voices to full choir, but the backing vocals can also be sung by a mixed group.

Starting

- Have your group speak and then sing the bass part in the first four bars (upper voices an octave higher than written). This will fix the groove and help singers to internalize the harmony.
- Now do the same with the backing vocals in the first four bars. The tone colour should be bright and smooth; vibrato, if used, should be relaxed and not wide.
- Now add the bass part, and feel free to click fingers on beats 2 and 4.

Teaching and rehearsing

- Continue with the bass and backing parts by teaching bars 9a–10a ('Hey, that's not cool'), 25a–26a ('Is this for real?'), and 41a–42a ('I'm out the door!'). Keep it clean and precise, and pay attention to the dynamics.
- To get that 'doo-wop' bass sound, ask your male singers to imagine that their cheeks are filled with sound. This tone is usually placed further back in the mouth and may sound 'untrained', but remember: doo-wop originated on the streets. Be careful, however—if the tone is too far back or 'swallowed', pitch problems may occur.
- Work through Ex. 1 to prepare for bars 17 and 33–4. Start slowly, then gradually build up the speed; listen out for tuning issues.
- Still on 'dee', practise bars 17 and 33–4, which conclude the bridge passages; now introduce bars 11–16 and 27–32, then sing each bridge complete. When this is secure, re-insert the words.

- Next, teach bars 10b–11 and 25b–26b ('hear what I say' and 'I'm not your pet'), then sing the whole piece with bass and backing vocals only.
- Now teach the solo to all the men, by rote in four-bar phrases. Start with the verses (bars 3–9, 19–25, and 35–41), then move on to the bridges (bars 11–18 and 27–34). Encourage the singers to tell a tale, and to interpret the lyrics using facial expressions and a comical tone colour.
- Finally, distribute your group among the parts, and sing the whole piece together.

Ideas

- Try adding a falsetto descant in the verses (see Ex. 2), maybe starting in bar 3 the second time through.
- Add some clicks on beats 2 and 4, but take them out for bars 10b–11 and 25b–26b.
- If the written pitch feels too high or low, experiment with the key.

Listen out

- Make sure the syncopated rhythms are tight against the pulse. Are the doo-wop syllables clear and rhythmic?
- Take care over descending intervals. These can easily cause the group to go flat if they are too wide.
- Listen to the balance. The bass part should be distinct from (and perhaps a bit louder than) the backing vocals, but it should never overpower the soloist.

Performing

- If you have a small ensemble, try a casual setting around the soloist—some sitting, some standing, etc. 'Side-steps', sways, or any other type of movement would work well for groups of all sizes, but stop or lessen the movement in bars 10b–11 and 25b–26b.
- Remember, tell the tale: let your audience in on the humour of this piece!

Ex. 1

Ex. 2

21 I'm Not Your Pet

Steve Milloy
additional words by John Moysen

Medium-fast doo-wop ♩ = 132

Lead

Backing vocals
Doom doom bah doom doom bah doom, ow ow.

Bass
Ba doom bah doom, bah doom, bah doom, ow ow. Ba doom bah

2b
(Solo(s) or small group)
The first time that I met - cha
think that you're a prin - cess

doom, ow ow. Doom doom bah doom doom bah

doom, ow ow. Ba doom bah doom, bah doom, bah

4
I thought that you were cool.
whose words I must o - bey.

But
So

doom, ow ow. Doom doom bah doom doom bah doom, ow ow.

doom, ow ow. Ba doom bah doom, bah doom, bah doom, ow ow. Ba doom bah

7
now ya got me think-in' that you took me for a fool.
girl you bet - ter lis - ten cos I'm 'bout to walk a -
Doom doom bah doom doom bah doom, ow ow. Hey, that's not
doom, bah doom, bah doom, ow ow. Ba doom bah doom. Hey, that's not
10a
You - way. I
cool. hear what I say. Ah,
cool. Ba doom bah doom, hear what I say. Ba doom bah doom bah doom bah
11
thought that it was sweet t' rub your tir - ed feet if
bop bah, bop bah,
doom. Doom bah doom bah doom, doom bah doom bah
13
you had a long ex - haust - in' day. If
bop bah, bop bah,
doom, doom bah doom bah doom bah doom bah doom bah doom bah

15
you'd just do the same   I would-n't feel so lame,   but
bop   bah,_____   bop   bah,_____
doom,   doom___ bah doom bah doom,   doom___ bah doom bah

17
f
you just scream at me: *mf*   You   catch your fav - 'rite pro-gramme
                                       not   your hi - red   ser - vant
f   (solo: comic, sassy!)   *mp*
you just scream at me: 'I wan-na watch T V!'   *mp*   Doom   doom bah doom doom bah
f
you just scream at me: Bah doom bah doom,   bah doom,   bah

20
while I make your fav - 'rite meal.   If
but you seem to for - get.   I'm
doom, ow ow.   Doom   doom bah doom doom bah doom, ow ow.
doom, ow ow. Bah doom bah doom,   bah doom,   bah doom, ow ow. Bah doom bah

23
[1
this is what you're of-f'rin',   it's a pret - ty lous - y deal.
not your faith - ful col - lie,   I'm your boy-friend not your
mf
Doom   doom bah doom doom bah doom, ow   ow,___   is this for
mf
doom,   bah doom,   bah doom, ow   ow.___   Ba doom bah doom, is this for

This page may be photocopied

26a
mf
2
I'm pet.
f
You
mf
real?
I'm not your pet.
mp
Ah,
mf
real? Ba doom bah doom, I'm not your pet.
Bah doom bah doom bah doom bah
27
tell me what to wear and how to comb my hair. This
bop bah, bop bah,
doom, doom bah doom bah doom, doom bah doom bah
29
twist - ed up Pyg - ma - lion is just too much to bear! I've
bop bah, bop bah,
doom, doom bah doom bah doom bah doom bah doom bah doom bah
31
had it up to here with all that you de-mand, so here's my fi-nal no-tice, on-ly
f
bop bah, bop bah, here's my fi-nal no-tice, on-ly
f
doom, doom bah doom bah doom, doom bah doom bah here's my fi-nal no-tice, on-ly

so much I can stand! I'm pack-in' all my stuff now
find your-self a but-ler,

so much I can stand! Doom doom bah doom doom bah

so much I can stand! Bah doom bah doom, bah doom, bah

an' head-in' out the door.
he'll make sure your needs are met.

Don't
The

doom, ow ow. Doom doom bah doom doom bah doom, ow ow.

doom, ow ow. Bah doom bah doom, bah doom, bah doom, ow ow. Bah doom bah

beg or try to stop me,
way you treat your boy-friends

I can't take it a-ny-
you'd do bet-ter with a

Doom doom bah doom doom bah doom, ow ow.

doom, bah doom, bah doom, ow ow. Ba doom bah

-more.

Go pet.

(dog sounds)

I'm out the door!

Go find a pet!

(dog sounds)

doom, I'm out the door! Ba doom bah doom, Go find a pet!

(dog sounds)

This page may be photocopied

Section III

Showstoppers

22 Come What May

RESOURCES ▶ CD1 track 22 (performance); CD2 track 21 (backing)

Information

This love duet was originally sung by Ewan McGregor and Nicole Kidman in the Hollywood blockbuster movie *Moulin Rouge* (2001). A 'big sing' ballad finale for any concert, it is guaranteed to get an audience on its feet. It is not difficult to learn the notes as there is much unison and two-part work, but it requires vocal stamina, sustained medium-to-high singing, and the ability to grade dynamics so as not to peak too soon. There are also opportunities for detailed phrasing and work on quiet, resonant singing in the first verse.

Starting

- Do some diaphragm exercises on a spoken 'huh'. Then throw your voice across the room to 'hah' and 'hay'. The sound should be bright, forward, and projected. Now turn this into 'come' and 'may'.
- Next, take a deep breath and make a sustained 'ss' sound. Feel the diaphragm working.
- Then combine the two. Sing 'come' on any note; start with a good 'k' sound and support the sound as if it were an 'ss'.
- Go back to 'hah', but this time add extra 'smile' and hint of 'eh' (like 'air') to your 'ah' sound. The sound should be focused, bright, and forward, so it will carry a long distance with minimum effort. Try 'come' and 'may' again.
- Next, reduce the power without reducing the support or the energy and brightness in the sound.
- Whisper the first line, 'Never knew I could feel like this', to the rhythm, and then mix a small amount of air with the sound—create a sung whisper, full of anticipation. (Beware of overdoing this effect, as it will dry out your throat and make the later singing tricky!)

Teaching and rehearsing

- The ending from bar 67 is tiring, so begin with the opening verse. Teach the words and pitches as they come, ensuring that word endings are clear. Aim for a soft but clear tone, with an element of whispered breathiness. Practise the cut-offs on 'this' (bar 6) and 'before' (bar 8)—the silences can be as expressive as the words.
- Once you get to bar 16, begin to add brightness to the sound using the 'hah'/'eh' idea above.
- Passing the line to and fro is a feature of this arrangement, and lines need to be sung as though one group is finishing the sentence of the other. It is important therefore to 'act' the words.

- Sing the 'Come what may' sections (beginning at bars 22, 48, and 67) side by side to practise the dynamics for each. The first can be quiet and tender throughout, the second comfortably projected but not too loud, and the third starts loud but must have headroom to grow.
- Rather than sing the whole song again and again, practise individual moments to save the voice.
- This song needs a conductor, at least at the end, where there are two pauses. The first (bar 77) is long and needs a clear cut-off and restart. The second (bar 78) is almost an extended *rall.* between 'dying' and 'day'. Here, the accompaniment almost stops, but the singers keep singing through to the end of the phrase. Give a clear downbeat at the 'a tempo' at the start of bar 79, and slow down again during bar 80. Enjoy the moment and indulge, but be very clear and don't take too long or the singers will expire!

Ideas

- In a warm up for a later rehearsal, practise singing very, very quietly so the opening is really magical. Sing the first phrase quietly, then half as loud, half as loud again, and finally so quietly that voices are on the edge of silence. Be demanding at both ends of the dynamic range.
- Explore vowel sounds in the final long loud 'Come what may' section. 'Come' and 'what' should be on an 'ah' sound; a really bright and efficient 'eh' on 'may' will also make it possible to be loud without strain.

Listen out

- Watch the balance at bars 63–4. The basses are at full stretch and need to be allowed to sing quietly without forcing the sound—most should be able to manage a low E♭ quietly. The other parts should judge their level by listening to the basses; if they can't hear them, they are too loud.
- Listen for tuning in the unison 'Come what may' at bar 22. You may need to rehearse the A–B♭–G line to make sure the B♭ is high enough and the A does not drop. Also check the vowel on 'may'—too dark and the pitch may drop.
- Aim for a blended sound in unison and octave singing, where no individual sticks out, and the group can get louder and softer as a unit by listening carefully and adjusting as they go. This is particularly important at the extremes of the dynamic range, where some will feel tempted to shout rather than sing loud in a controlled way.

Performing

- With fewer singers, watch that a big piano does not drown the voices in louder sections; with larger numbers or even a massed group, the piano may need to play up slightly in the quieter sections. Also beware of the tendency to lead from the piano in 'teacher–pianist' mode. This can be habitual, particularly if you lead class singing, and will lead to a tendency to play louder than the choir sings. Be audible, but let the singers lead.

- If you are using the backing track, run the whole song several times so the singers become familiar with the tempo. You will also need to practise the end a number of times. At the performance, make sure the balance between backing and singers is well judged, and that singers can clearly hear the track. You might consider using foldback speakers, pointing at the choir. If you have the resources, think about miking the choir up too, so you can bring the volume up and down in the mix.

22 Come What May

David Baerwald
arr. Charles Beale

7
like I've ne-ver seen the sky__ be-fore, want to van-ish in-
C/B♭
B♭
/A
Gm7
p
10
- side__ your kiss, ev-'ry day I love you more and more.
Gm11
C7
B♭sus
B♭
/A
13
mp
Lis-ten to__ my heart can you hear it sing? Tell-ing me_ to give___ you
Gm
C7sus
C7
F7sus
mp

ev - 'ry-thing, sea-sons may change winter_ to spring, to spring. But I

spring._____

spring, to spring.

love you_ un - til the end_____ of time. Come what

_ may, come what_ may I will

love you un-til my dy - ing__ day._____

Brighter

T. & B. *unis.*

Sud-den-ly the world_____ seems such a per - fect place,

S. & A. *unis.*

Sud-den-ly it moves with such_ a per - fect_ grace,

sud-den-ly my life does-n't seem____ such a waste.____

It all re-volves a-round you____ and there's no moun - tain_ too high, no

ri - ver too wide, sing out_ this song and I'll be there by your side,_

43
mp
ah!
storm clouds may ga - ther_ and stars may col - lide_ ah!
p
But I
Gm /F Gm C9sus C9
p
Ped.
46
p
I love you till the end of time. Come what
love you_ un - til the
f
f
Bb/F Eb/F Bb/F F7 Bb F/A
49
_ may,_ come what_ may_ I will
Gm F/G C7 Bb/C
f

53
love you until my dying day. Oh come what
Bbadd2 Bb Bb6/F F7 Bb Fadd2/A F/A
56
ff
may, come what may
Gm C9sus
59
I will love you.
Sud-den-ly the world seems
love you, will love you.
C9 Bb/C Cm/Bb Am7(b5)/D Ebmaj9 Cm9
p

63
such a per-fect place.
Bb/C
Ebmaj9
pp
f
Ped.
8va bassa
66
ff
Come what_ may,
come what
ff
Gb
Ab
Bbadd2
Bb
Eb/Bb
Bb
Bbadd2 Bb
ff
70
_ may,
come what_ may,
come what
Eb/Bb
Bb
F/Bb
Bb
Eb/Bb
Bb
F/Bb
Bb

slower
very broad
74
may
I will love you
un - til my
Eb/Bb Eb/A Gm Gm7 /F Ebmaj7 nc Eb
a tempo
molto rall.
78
dy - ing day! Come what may.
Bb/F F7 Bb Gb Fm/Ab Bbadd2 Bb

22 Come What May

Vocal score

David Baerwald
arr. Charles Beale

Hollywood ballad – with utter conviction ♩ = 65

(Piano introduction)

unis. p

Ne-ver knew I could feel like this, like I've ne-ver seen the sky

___ be-fore, want to van-ish in - side your kiss, ev-'ry day I love you

mp

more and more. Lis-ten to_ my heart can you hear it sing? Tell-ing me to give_ you

**S.
A.**

spring.____

ev - 'ry-thing, sea - sons_ may change win - ter___ to spring, to

spring.____

**T.
B.**

spring, to

p *mp*

spring.
___

But I love you_ un - til the end____ of time. Come what

p *mp*

spring.

This page may be photocopied

Brighter

S. & A. unis.

T. & B. unis.

may, — come what — may — I will

love — you un-til my dy - ing — day.

sud-den-ly it moves with such a

Sud-den-ly the world seems such a per-fect place,

per - fect grace, sud-den-ly my life does-n't seem — such a waste. —

Lyrics beneath the music:

m. 37–38: It all re-volves a-round you_____ and there's no moun-

m. 39–41: -tain_ too high, no ri-ver too wide, sing out this song and I'll be

m. 42–44: there by your side,_

(lower voice) storm clouds may ga-ther_ and stars may col-lide_

m. 45–47:
(upper) ah! I love you till the end of time. Come what
(lower) ah! But I love you_ un-til the

This page may be photocopied

Lyrics under the music:

may, _____ come what ___ may _____ I will

love __ you un-til my dy - ing day. Oh come what ___ may, _____

___ come what may _____ I will love you.

love you, will love you.

Sud-den-ly the world seems such a per-fect place. _____

Come what may, come what
may, come what may, come what
may I will love you un-til my
dy-ing day! Come what may.

23 Pages

RESOURCES ▶ CD1 track 23 (performance); CD2 track 22 (backing)

Information

This is a lyrical and uplifting song in a 'folk pop' style, whose words are an expression of thanks to a special person. Written in three parts, with plenty of unison and two-part writing, this song is instantly singable and your group will pick it up quickly. It could be used for assemblies, church services, or as a general 'thank you' to your audience.

Starting

- Encourage a warm, natural tone by singing some 'mm–ng–ah' exercises (see p. xii). Singers should aim for evenness of tone throughout their range.
- In a key to suit the group, make up some scale exercises on a single vowel; aim to maintain the brightness of the top of the voice as you go lower.

Teaching and rehearsing

- At a steady tempo, speak the verses. Pay particular attention to the rhythm, which should have a slight bounce and lift.
- Now teach the same passages part by part and then sing together, keeping the sound warm and smooth with a natural ebb and flow in the dynamics.
- Look at the chorus and notice the movement of the melody: in bar 18 it switches from alto to baritone, and then moves back to alto in bar 19. As you teach the parts, make sure the melody is predominant.
- The chorus should have a brighter, fuller tone quality each time it returns, with the apex being bars 37–44. The following chorus is more subdued and personal.
- The bridge (from 'Ev-'ry word is a whisper . . .') should be both the quietest and the most energized part of the piece. At 'Each chapter's a kiss', begin a steady crescendo to 'cry' (bar 27), taking note of the *fp*. Come back down at bar 28 and build again to bar 35, slightly exaggerating the *fp*.
- The tag (upbeat to bar 53 to the end) should be warm and subdued, with a slightly breathy tone.

Ideas

- Use the optional notes in bars 35–6 to enrich the harmony.
- Give your group a feel for the 'folk pop' style by listening to Kelly Clarkson's 'Breakaway', 'Piano Man' by Billy Joel, and 'Norwegian Wood' by the Beatles.

Listen out

- To help with tuning, check that vowel sounds are consistent throughout the group, e.g. in the word 'love' in bars 29–36.
- Keep the bridge steady and in tempo. Repetition has a tendency to be rushed.

Performing

- Before singing, ask each member of the group to think of a person they are proud to have in their life, and to incorporate that feeling into their performance.

23 Pages

Words: John Moysen
Music: Steve Milloy

Acoustic rock feel, with a lilt ♩. = 57

1. 'f I put pen to pa - per to write_ of my life (For we've
2. With - out you my life_ has no rea - son or rhyme And I

Lyrics:

all got a sto - ry to tell), _ Your name would ap-pear on the
don't have a sto - ry to give; _ With you all the piec - es fall

cov - er, _ On each page, ev - 'ry sen-tence as _ well. _
in - to line And you give me a rea - son to _ live. _

Chorus
mf
(mel.) Oh, the book _ of my life _ goes through sta - ges, And my most

Chord symbols:
/G   /F   Ebsus2   Bbsus2/G   /A

Bbsus2   /A   /G   /F   Fsus/Eb   F/Eb

Fsus/Eb   F/Eb   Fsus/Eb   Fsus   Bbsus2   /D   /Eb   /F

mf

loy - al read - er is you. You're the one___ who keeps turn - ing the pag-

-es; You're the one___ that I keep turn-ing to.

to. Ev-'ry word is a whis - per, each

sen-tence a sigh.   Each chap-ter's a kiss,___   a cry___ (mel.)

Each chap-ter's a kiss,   ev-'ry page is a cry___

E♭   Fadd4/E♭   E♭   Fadd4/E♭   B♭add2/D   Cm7(add11)

love,___   love,___

of   love,   love,

love,   love,

B♭sus2/D   E♭   F/E♭   E♭   F/E♭

love,___   love,___   love,___

love,   love,   love,

love,___   love,___   love,___

E♭   F/E♭   E♭   F/E♭   E♭   F/E♭

love,___   love,___   love,___

34
— love, love!
fp
Chorus
f
(mel.)
love, love!
fp
Oh, the book
— love!
f
E♭ F/E♭ E♭ F/E♭ E♭ F/E♭ E♭ F9sus
f
37
— of my life goes through sta - ges, And my most loy - al read - er is
B♭sus2 /D /E♭ /F /G /F
40
(mel.)
you. You're the one who keeps turn - ing the pag - es; You're the one
(mel.)
/E♭ /F B♭sus2 /D /E♭ /F

43
mf
that I keep turn-ing to. Oh, the book of my life through the
mf
/G /F E♭sus2 B♭sus2 /D
46
ag - es Is the tale of a heart ev - er true. For it's you
(mel.)
(mel.)
/E♭ /F /G /F E♭sus2
49
that keeps turn - ing the pag - es, And it's you that I keep turn-ing
B♭sus2 /D /E♭ /F /G /F

52
mp
to.
Each page is a state-ment of
Each page is a state-ment of love. Each
Eb F/Eb Eb F/Eb Eb F/Eb
mp

55
1
2
love. Each love.
page is a state - ment of page is a state - ment of love.
Eb F/Eb Eb F/Eb Ebadd2

23 Pages

Vocal score

Words: John Moysen
Music: Steve Milloy

Acoustic rock feel, with a lilt ♩. = 57

(Piano introduction)

S.
A.

Bar.

mp

mp

1. 'f I
2. With -

(mel.)

put pen to pa - per to write_ of my life (For we've all got a sto - ry to tell),
-out you my life_ has no rea - son or rhyme And I don't have a sto - ry to give;

Your name would ap - pear on the cov - er,_____ On each
With you all the piec - es fall in - to line And you

Chorus

mf

(mel.)

page, ev - 'ry sen - tence as_____ well._____ Oh, the book
give me a rea - son to_____ live._____

mf

This page may be photocopied

16
— of my life — goes through sta - ges, And my most — loy - al read - er is
19
(mel.)
you. You're the one — who keeps turn - ing the pag - es; You're the one
(mel.)
22
1
— that I keep — turn - ing to.
23b
2
p
to. Ev-'ry word is a whis - per, each sen-tence a sigh.
(mel.)
p
Each
26
fp
(mel.)
sub. p
Each chap - ter's a kiss, — a cry — of
fp
chap - ter's a kiss, — ev - 'ry page is a cry —

29
love, love, love,
p mp
love, love, love,
p mp
love, love, love,
32
love, love, love, love!
mf fp
love, love, love,
mf fp
love, love, love!
36
Chorus
f
(mel.)
Oh, the book of my life goes through sta - ges, And my most
f
39
loy - al read - er is you. You're the one who keeps turn - ing the pag-
(mel.)
(mel.)

es; You're the one___ that I keep turn-ing to. Oh, the book

___ of my life_ through the ag - es Is the tale___ of a heart ev - er

true. (mel.) For it's you___ that keeps turn-ing the pag - es, And it's you
(mel.)

___ that I keep turn-ing to. Each

Each page is a state-ment of___

page is a state-ment of_ love. Each love._____

love. Each page is a state-ment of_ page is a state-ment of_ love.

This page may be photocopied

24 Comedy Tonight

RESOURCES ▶ CD2 track 1 (performance) and 23 (backing)

Information

Written as a late entry to the 1962 musical *A Funny Thing Happened on the Way to the Forum*, this energetic show tune has been taken out of its original setting and given a more contemporary rhythmic treatment. On one level, this fun song is about the importance of being entertaining, but like many Stephen Sondheim songs it also uses irony in a sophisticated way to be critical of those who are purely comical.

Starting

- The sopranos have a wider range than the other parts. Warm up all your singers with the following exercises, rising in pitch with each repetition to expand the register.

ha   ha   ha   ha   ha   *etc.*

ee___ oh___ ee___ oh___   ee   *etc.*

- Because of its clever lyrics, this piece offers many opportunities for acting with the face, body, and voice. Have your singers sing a G major chord in root, 1st, or 2nd position to a vowel of their choice, and display these emotions: bright and engaging, loud and raucous, warm and inviting, confident and authoritative, hushed and excited, repulsed, etc. Try some of your own!

Teaching and rehearsing

- At a slow and steady tempo, starting with four- and working up to eight-bar phrases, teach the lyrics and rhythm of bars 7–42. Keep the pronunciation clean and conversational, and the long notes energized. Steadily accelerate the tempo with each successful run-through.
- In the same fashion, teach the melody (Soprano line) of this section, using 'bup' and 'buh-duh' for short notes and 'bah' for long notes. Aim for a bright, full tone and a normal to fast vibrato; make sure lower notes are not pushed or forced. Pay attention to the leap from bar 11–12, making sure each voice is supported and singing with ease. Take care that the descending intervals in bar 12 aren't too wide.
- Keep the tone relaxed and bright in the higher register through bar 29; again, watch the intervals as voices descend.

- Now teach the parts in bars 7–42, with particular attention to the bass in bars 12–14. Ask the basses to sing G–F–G–F♯ back and forth, listening out for the tuning between F and F♯. Practice bars 25–9 slowly to refine tuning, and make sure faces and voices are alive and full of energy, especially in bars 35–41.
- Next, sing the written lyrics. Are the vowel sounds consistent? Pronounce the words as for a Broadway or West End audience—crisply, somewhere between conversational and standard English.
- In two- to four-bar phrases, teach bars 50–65, incorporating the 'quick-change' acting skills worked on in 'Starting'. Vary the tone as you progress through the piece: e.g. bars 74–5 could be rich and classical-sounding, and 76–7 might be straight and bright. In bar 78, return to a 'show chorus' sound (bright, full tone, and normal to fast vibrato).
- In bars 84–7, allow the moving parts to shine through, but ensure the energy is maintained on the held notes.

Ideas

- Discuss the group's favourite comedians. Who and what makes everyone laugh? Keep the answers in mind when singing the song.
- Search the Internet for videos of this song. What do you like about each one, and what would you change? Consider adding some movement to your performance.

Listen out

- This song has some wide ranges, so make sure singers are using good support and avoiding muscle strain to sing higher and lower notes.
- Are the basses' F♮ and F♯ pitches accurate in bars 13–14?
- Check bars 74–7, which require singers to switch tone quality at the drop of a hat.
- Make sure your singers take in a good amount of air before 'tonight' in bar 89. Hold this note to the end, giving it a little push and crescendo in bars 94–5. Men and Sopranos may want to use a little more head voice and less chest voice, while keeping the sound bright and energized.

Performing

- Even if no movement is incorporated into your performance, let the lyrics show on your faces and in your bodies. Act it out and have fun!

24 Comedy Tonight

Stephen Sondheim
arr. Steve Milloy

Upbeat show style; tongue-in-cheek ♩ = 129

Lyrics:
Some-thing fa - mi - liar, some-thing pe - cu - liar, some-thing for ev -'ry one a com-e-dy to - night! Some-thing ap - peal - ing, some-thing ap - pall - ing,

19
something for ev - 'ry one a com-e-dy to - night!
No-thing with kings,
Gadd2 Fadd2 D G C6/D G
25
no-thing with crowns, bring on the lov - ers, li - ars and clowns.
B F#m7 B Am7 Gadd2/B C7 Gadd2/B Am7 Dsus
31
Old sit - u - a - tions, new com - pli - ca - tions, no-thing por - ten-tous or po -
Gadd2 Am7/G Gadd2 Am7/G Gadd2

37
f
- lite; tragedy tomorrow, comedy to -
Ebsus Eb7 Am7 Bm7 C/D D
42
- night!
Gadd2 Am7/G Gadd2 G5 Ab5 Aadd2 E7sus/A
ff sub. mp
48
unis. mf
Something convulsive,
something repulsive,
Aadd2 E7sus/A Aadd2 E7+ Aadd2 E7+
mp

54
unis. mf
something for ev - 'ry one a com-e-dy to-night!
oo!
unis. mp
Some-thing es - the-tic,
Aadd2
Gadd2
E
Aadd2
E7sus/A
60
some-thing fre - net-ic, some-thing for ev - 'ry one a com-e-dy to-night!
oo oo oo!
A9
E7
E7(♭9)
Aadd2
Gadd2
E
66
no-thing of Fate, weight-y af - fairs will
No-thing of Gods,
A
D6/E
A
C#
G#m7
C#
Bm7
C#m7

72
mp
f
just have to wait.
No-thing that's for - mal,
no-thing that's nor - mal,
Dadd2
Bm7
E
A
D/A
E7/B
A
Bm7(♭5)
E
78
mp
f
no rec - i - ta-tions to re - cite!
O-pen up the cur - tain! A
p
A
Aadd2
mf
Fsus
F7
Bm7
C#m7
84
unis. p
com-e-dy, com-e-dy, com-e-dy, com - e - dy,
com-e - dy,
com-e-dy, com-e-dy, com-e-dy, com-e - dy,
D/E
p

com-e-dy   to - night!

To - night!

24 Comedy Tonight

Vocal score

Stephen Sondheim
arr. Steve Milloy

Upbeat show style; tongue-in-cheek ♩ = 129

(Piano introduction)

Some-thing fa - mi-liar, some-thing pe - cu-liar, some-thing for ev-'ry one a

com-e-dy to - night! Some-thing ap - peal - ing, some-thing ap - pall - ing,

some-thing for ev - 'ry one a com-e-dy to - night!

No-thing with kings,

25
no-thing with crowns, bring on the lov - ers, li - ars and clowns.
31
mp
Old sit - u - a - tions, new com - pli - ca - tions, no-thing por - ten-tous or po -
mp
37
f
- lite; tragg-e - dy to - mor - row, com-e - dy to -
f
42
- night!

50 unis. mf
Some-thing con - vul-sive,
unis. mf
some-thing re - pul-sive,
some-thing for ev - 'ry one a
56 f
com-e-dy to - night!
unis. mp
oo!
f
some-thing fre - net-ic,
unis. mp
Some-thing es - the-tic,
oo oo oo!
62 mf
f
some-thing for ev - 'ry one a com-e-dy to - night!
No-thing of Gods,
68
no-thing of Fate, weight-y af - fairs will just have to wait.

Lyrics under the music:

No-thing that's for-mal, no-thing that's nor-mal, no rec-i-ta-tions to re-cite!_____ O-pen up the cur-tain!

A com-e-dy,_____
A com-e-dy, com-e-dy, com-e-dy, com-e-dy,_

com-e-dy, com-e-dy, com-e-dy, com-e-dy, com-e-dy to-night!_____

To-night!

25 Hot Hot Hot

RESOURCES ▶ CD2 track 2 (performance) and 24 (backing)

☐ Information

This calypso tune is an ideal show-closer and crowd-pleaser. A favourite of wedding bands and footballers everywhere, it was a hit for Alphonsus Cassell (aka Arrow), as well as for the singer David Johansen in his 'Buster Poindexter' persona. It's a high-energy song all about celebrating!

☐ Starting

- Warm up the body to a calypso beat, perhaps using the backing track. Start with the shoulders, rolling them back and forth, then let shoulders and arms bounce. Rotate wrists and shake out hands. Now turn the upper body from side to side, then rotate your knees, alternating from left to right. Finally, standing on tiptoe, stretch high with arms above the head, then flop down like a rag doll and slowly roll downward until your upper body is as far down as it will comfortably go. Hold and relax. Then slowly roll upward and shake it all out.
- Clap the rhythm of 'Hot hot hot' against a stamped crotchet/quarter-note pulse (approx. ♩ = 120). Try clapping only two out of the three notes: the first then the last; the first then the second; or the second then the third.
- Establish a bright, energized vocal tone on a single note, and sing 'Hot hot hot' in rhythm—keep it tight and clean.
- Divide into three or four groups. Starting at about ♩ = 87, and working up to ♩ = 120, build up this drum-kit exercise part by part.

Now, using call and response, chant the lyrics of bars 54–61 over this backing.

☐ Teaching and rehearsing

- Start by setting a party mood! Have some of your group perform the drum-kit exercise above, and teach bars 54–61 call and response style.
- Teach the opening 'olé's in the same fashion, building part by part.
- Speak bars 18–24. Once the rhythm is solid, teach the notes for each part separately then sing it together. Sing in a bright 'belt' with minimal vibrato to create an 'island' sound.
- Next, speak bars 25–9, with the upper and lower parts as separate groups. Then teach the notes for each part separately as before, and sing it together.
- Teach bars 30–40 and 66–end in the same fashion. Give the triplets (bar 66 onwards) a stretched feel to keep them from becoming too short.
- You might want to try singing with a Caribbean accent. For ideas, listen to the recordings suggested below, or to the CD demo.
- Add in bars 46–61, learnt earlier, and sing the whole piece.

☐ Ideas

- Get performance ideas by listening to the original recording by Arrow, as well as the famous version by Buster Poindexter. Although basically the same song performed in the same style, David Johansen puts on a character—Buster Poindexter—whereas Arrow is simply being himself. What similarities or differences do you notice? What could you incorporate into your performance?
- Invite your group to 'party' during the instrumental sections: shout, dance, and maybe even start a conga-line! Listen to the CD for ideas.

☐ Listen out

- Check that the song doesn't rush, and ensure that the rhythm and words are clean and precise—e.g. in bars 20 (and similar), 22–3, 33, and 54–61.
- Be wary of over-singing. Your singers should aim to achieve an energetic 'party vibe' by maintaining a precise and punchy sound rather than shouting, which can damage the voice and affect blend and precision. Perhaps ask singers to check their voices for any pain or hoarseness during or immediately after rehearsal. Listen for any louder, more confident voices sticking out.

☐ Performing

- Create a party spirit! Maybe even parade your conga-line through the audience and invite them to join in!

25 Hot Hot Hot

Alphonsus Cassell
arr. Steve Milloy

Fast calypso; celebration time! ♩ = 120

O - lé o - lé o - lé o - lé, o - lé o - lé o - lé o - lé.

Me mind on fi - re, me soul on fi - re, feel-in' hot hot hot.
See peo - ple rock-in', hear peo-ple chant-in', feel-in' hot hot hot.

Par-ty peo-ple all a-round me feel-in'
Keep up the spir-it, come on let's do it, feel-in'

hot hot hot.
hot hot hot.

Hot hot hot.

Uh what to do on a night like
It's in the air, cel-e - bra-tion

Hot hot hot._   Hot hot hot._   Hot hot hot._   We

this?   Mu-sic sweet,_____ I__ can't re - sist.
time!   Mu-sic sweet,_____ cap-ti-vate your mind.   We

need_____ a - par-ty song,   a   fun -   da - men-tal
have_____ this par-ty song,   this fun -   da - men-tal

charm,   so we can room boom boom boom!   Yeah, we
charm,

room boom boom boom!

Feel-in' hot hot hot.

Feel-in' hot hot hot.

O -

46

-lé o - lé o - lé o - lé, o - lé o - lé o - lé o - lé. O-

f

50

-lé o - lé o - lé o - lé, o - lé o - lé o - lé o - lé.

Bb   Eb   F   Bb   Bb   Eb   F   Bb

f

54

unis. *f* (spoken)

Peo-ple in the par - ty, hot hot hot.

unis. *f* (spoken)

Peo-ple in the par - ty, hot hot hot.

they

They come to the par-ty know-in' what they got.

come to the par-ty know-in' what they got.

I'm hot, you're hot. He's hot, she's hot. I'm hot, you're hot.

He's hot, she's hot.

Bb   F   Bb

f

Hot hot hot. How you feel-in'?

How you feel-in'?

Hot hot hot.

F   Bb   F

68
Hot hot hot. How you feel-in'? Hot hot hot.
How you feel-in'? Hot hot hot.
B♭ F B♭

71
Hot hot hot. Hot hot hot. Hot hot hot.
F B♭ F B♭

25 Hot Hot Hot

Vocal score

Alphonsus Cassell
arr. Steve Milloy

Fast calypso; celebration time! ♩ = 120

S.
A.

O - lé o - lé o - lé o - lé, o - lé o - lé o - lé o - lé.

T.
B.

12 unis. *mf*

Me mind on fi - re, me soul on fi - re, feel-in' hot hot hot.
See peo-ple rock-in', hear peo-ple chant-in', feel-in' hot hot hot.

12 unis.

mf

Par - ty peo-ple all a-round me feel-in'
Keep up the spir-it, come on let's do it, feel-in'

unis.

hot hot hot. Hot hot hot.
hot hot hot.

unis.

Uh what to do_____ on a night like
It's in the air,_____ cel-e-bra-tion

This page may be photocopied

Hot hot hot._ Hot hot hot._ Hot hot hot._ We

this? Mu-sic sweet,_____ I__ can't re - sist.
time! Mu-sic sweet,_____ cap-ti-vate your mind.

We

need_____ a - par - ty song, a fun - da - men - tal
have_____ this par - ty song, this fun - da - men - tal

charm, so we can room boom boom boom! Yeah, we
charm,

room boom boom boom! Feel - in' hot hot hot.

Feel-in' hot hot hot.

O - lé o - lé o - lé o - lé, o - lé o - lé o -

-lé o - lé. O - lé o - lé o - lé o - lé, o - lé o - lé o - lé o - lé.

unis. **f** (spoken)
Peo-ple in the par - ty, hot hot hot.

unis. **f** (spoken)
Peo-ple in the par - ty, hot hot hot.
they

They come to the par-ty know-in' what they got.

come to the par-ty know-in' what they got.

This page may be photocopied

Measure 58:
I'm hot, you're hot. He's hot, she's hot. I'm hot, you're hot. He's hot, she's hot.

Measure 62:
Hot hot hot.
How you feel-in'?

Measure 67:
How you feel-in'?   Hot hot hot. How you feel-in'?
Hot hot hot. How you feel-in'?   Hot hot hot.

Measure 70:
Hot hot hot. Hot hot hot. Hot hot hot. Hot hot hot.

26 Dancing in the Street

RESOURCES ▶ CD2 track 3 (performance) and 25 (backing)

▢ Information

This infectious song was made famous by Martha and the Vandellas in 1964, and it is one of the best examples of the Detroit-based 1960s pop style Motown. An international hit, it reached number 2 in the US Billboard charts and number 5 in the UK in 1969, and has been covered by many pop artists, perhaps most notably Mick Jagger and David Bowie in 1985. Its celebratory, upbeat tone also has a political edge—in true 60s fashion, music can solve the problems of the world. This song was written for a soloist and three backing singers; in this arrangement, the register has been lowered slightly to make it accessible to SATB groups.

▢ Starting

- Warm up with some body work (stretching, relaxing, moving) and rhythm. Establish a pulse of ♩ = 116 and clap on beats 2 and 4, and then on 2 and the 'and' of 2 and 4. Ensure hips, knees, and elbows are not locked, and sway from side to side while singing.
- Sing the opening phrase, aiming for tight rhythm and clear articulation. Then proceed up in semitones. Ensure the lowest final note is energized right through to the end. Work on keeping the 'ah' sound bright and forward in the mouth.
- Divide into three parts, and sing the opening chord of 'dancin' in the street' in bar 15 on A, C, and F. Use urban-American vowel pronunciation, e.g. the 'a' in 'dancin'' should sound as in 'hat', rather than as in 'car'.
- Get a groove going and sing the phrase round and round on bars 15–16, making sure it is blended and tight. After four repetitions, go up a semitone and repeat. Repeat again, going up in further semitones, listening for accurate tuning. Try this going up in tones too.

▢ Teaching and rehearsing

- Begin by simply saying the rhythm and the words, aiming for neat phrasing and accurate, natural-sounding word stresses.
- If you are using a soloist, teach them the part from bar 12 first, and do the same with the bass solo at bar 22ff. If not, a group of sopranos or top-line singers should take this part.
- Then teach each section in order, possibly leaving the introductory four bars until later.
- On initial hearing, this song can seem repetitive because the groove stays the same for much of the material.

Identify sections as A (bar 5), B (bar 13, same chords but question and answer) and C (bar 19, change in harmony—Bridge). Verse 2 then begins at bar 35, with the men singing the melody.
- Watch for doubly struck vowels such as 'bea - eat' (bar 8) and 'ri - ight' (bar 10). They take a little getting used to but are essential to the rhythmic character and add to the groove by re-asserting the pulse in the middle of a vowel.
- Teach the scoops, slides, and inflections as part of the line—don't add them in later as afterthoughts.

▢ Ideas

- In the style, a dance routine would add to the impact of the performance. Invent your own according to the level of your group, or research original 1960s videos of groups of this time on TV clip websites. Martha and the Vandellas, the Four Tops, and the Temptations are all good starting-points. Include your routine in bars 54–7—there is also scope for some vocal improvising—or wherever you choose.
- If you can, try experimenting with a slightly higher key to add impact. Avoid strain.

▢ Listen out

- Bar 19 (on the repeat) is an arrival point after an extended F groove. Check dynamics here, and enjoy the groove and feel the tension build before the climactic arrival on B♭. Check the syncopated positioning of words ahead of the beat, such as 'what you wear' (bars 27–8) and 'they'll be dancing' (bars 34–5).
- Check the division of the altos in bars 35 and 57; the tenors in bar 61; and the sopranos briefly at bar 65b. If doublings are not possible in your group, allocate notes in the chord to different sections.
- In bar 42, aim for a natural sound rather than a strict triplet.
- If the E♭ in bar 5 etc. is too high, try singing the Mixolydian mode on F, with a major 3rd and a flattened 7th.
- Listen for the balance between the melody and backings, particularly where the melody travels between voices. If using microphones, this can be solved in the mix, but ensure the singers are aware of where the focus is at each point in the song, especially when the melody travels between voices.
- Tight backing vocals was a feature of the original Motown tracks. Work on this by ear, ensuring that as they get tighter they maintain energy and individuality.

▣ Performing

- Question and answer singing between men and women features strongly here. Differentiate between the positions of the two groups, possibly with each facing slightly inwards.
- The performance style is that of pop or gospel music. Clapping should involve the audience, so get them up on their feet! Feet can step from side to side and involve knees, hips, and shoulders too, to avoid stiffness.
- Bright eyes and engaged faces will also add to the effect—remember to perform to your audience and speak to them directly. Eyes can cover the room consciously, so everyone feels included. Try also 'talking' to individuals you know—and even some you don't—as this will personalize the performance.

26 Dancing in the Street

William Stevenson,
Marvin Gaye, and Ivy Hunter
arr. Charles Beale

the wo-orld, are you rea-dy for a brand new bea - eat?

Eb/F   F7   Eb/F   F7   Eb/F   F7

Sum-mer's here_ and the time is ri - ight for danc - in' a in the street.

Eb/F   F7   Eb/F   F7   Eb/F   F7

S.

(opt. solo)

They're danc-in' in Chi-ca - go_   Down in

A.

danc-in' in the street

T.
B.

danc-in' in the street

Eb/F   F7   F   Bb/C   F   Eb/F   F7

15
New Or - leans
In New York_ Ci - ty
All_
danc-in' in the street
danc-in' in the street
danc-in' in the street
danc-in' in the street
F Bb/C F Eb/F F7 F Bb/C F
18
(mf)
— we need___ is mu - sic, sweet mu - sic, There'll be
sweet sweet sweet sweet mu - sic
sweet sweet sweet sweet mu - sic
Bb/F F7 Bb7 F

21
(end solo)
S.
mu - sic ev - ery-where
oo oo oo
A.
ah
ev-ery - where
oo oo oo
T.
ah
ev-ery - where
oo oo oo
(opt. solo)
3
B.
ah
ev-ery - where. There'll be swing - in', sway - in', and
Bb7
F7
Eb/F
F7
24
S.
A.
unis.
oo
danc-in' in the street
Oh!
T.
oo
danc-in' in the street
Oh!
(end solo)
B.
re-cords play - in', danc - in' a in the street!
Oh!
Eb/F
F7
Eb/F
F7
Eb/F
F

27
S.
A.
It does-n't mat-ter what you wear, just as long as you are there, So come on
mp
unis.
T.
B.
ah ah So come on,
A7
Dm
last time to Coda
31
cresc.
unis.
ah
Ev-ery-where a-round the world
cresc.
f
ev-ery guy grab a girl Ev-ery-where a-round the world There'll be danc-
last time to Coda
Gm7
Bb/C
cresc.
f
35
f
div.
danc-in' in the street
danc-in' in the street
- in', they're danc-in' in the stree - eet.
Eb/F
F7
Eb/F
F7
Eb/F
F7

38
oo oo oo
oo oo oo
This is an in - vi - ta - tion a - cross the na - tion, a
Eb/F F7 Eb/F F7 Eb/F F7
41
oo
3
chance for folks to mee - eet. There'll be laugh - in', sing - in', and
Eb/F F7 Eb/F F7 Eb/F F7
44
unis. mf
Danc-in' in the stree - eet, Phil-a-del-phia P A -
mu-sic swing-in', Danc - in' a in the stree - eet.
Eb/F F7 Eb/F F7 Eb/F F7
mf

47
- ee, Bal - ti-more and D C now,
mf
Phil - a - del-phia P A - ee, Bal - ti-more and D C
Eb/F F7 Eb/F F7 Eb/F F7
50
(S. only)
Can't for-get the mo-tor ci - ty. All we need is mu -
mp
now, ah
Eb/F F7 F F7
CODA
opt. vocal improvising and/or dance routine
53
(first time only)
clap
f
the world There'll be danc - in'
the world There'll be danc - in'
F7

(last time only)
x 4
56
div.
oo oo oo
oo oo oo
danc-in' in the street
x 4
F7
Bb/C
F7
60
oo
Come on now!
Danc-in' in the street
danc-in' in the street
div. oo oo oo
oo oo oo
Bb/C F7
Bb/C F7
64
1
2
ff
danc-in' in the street
div.
oo oo oo
danc-in' in the street.
Yeah!
oo
Come on now!
ff
Bb/C F7
1
2 F
F/C Bb/C F
ff

26 Dancing in the Street

Vocal score

William Stevenson,
Marvin Gaye, and Ivy Hunter
arr. Charles Beale

Motown rock; fun 'n' funky ♩ = 116

bup bup bu-di-yup bah!_____ bup bup bu-di-yup bah!_____ Call-

- in' out_ a-round_ the wo-orld, are you rea-dy for a brand new bea-eat?

Sum-mer's here_ and the time is ri-ight for danc-in' a in the street.

(opt. solo)

They're danc-in' in Chi-ca - go_ Down in New Or - leans

danc-in' in the street danc-in' in the street

danc-in' in the street danc-in' in the street

This page may be photocopied

In New York Ci - ty

All____ we need is mu - sic, sweet mu-

danc-in' in the street

sweet sweet

danc-in' in the street

sweet sweet

- sic, There'll be mu-sic ev - ery-where oo oo oo____

sweet sweet mu - sic ah_____ ev-ery-where oo oo oo____

sweet sweet mu - sic ah_____ ev-ery-where oo oo oo____

sweet sweet mu - sic ah_____ ev-ery-where. There'll be swing-in', sway-in', and

oo_____ danc-in' in the street Oh!__

oo_____ danc-in' in the street Oh!__

re-cords play - in', danc - in' a in the street! Oh!__

System — S.A. / T.B.

27

S.A.: It does-n't mat-ter what you wear, just as long as you are there,____ So come on

T.B.: *mp* ah_____ ah_____ So come on,

31 *cresc.*

S.A.: ah_____ *unis.* Ev-ery-where a-round the world

T.B.: *cresc.* ev-ery guy grab a girl_ Ev-ery-where a-round the world There'll be danc-

last time **to Coda** ⊕

35 *f*

S.A.: *div.* danc-in' in the street danc-in' in the street

T.B.: - in', they're danc-in' in the stree - eet.

38

S.A.: oo oo oo_____ oo____ oo oo

T.B.: This is an in - vi-ta - tion a-cross the na - tion, a

41

S.A.: oo

T.B.: chance for folks to mee - eet. There'll be ⌐3¬ laugh - in', sing - in', and

44
mf unis.
Danc-in' in the stree - eet, Phil - a - del-phia P A -
mu - sic swing - in', Danc - in' a in the stree - eet.
47
- ee, Bal - ti-more and D C___ now,
mf
Phil - a - del-phia P A - ee, Bal - ti-more and D C__
50
(S. only)
Can't for - get the mo - tor ci - ty. All___ we need__ is mu -
mp
__ now, ah
CODA
opt. vocal improvising and/or dance routine
53
f
(first time only)
clap
__ the world There'll be danc - in'
__ the world There'll be danc - in'
56
(last time only)
x 4
div.
oo oo oo___ oo__ oo oo
danc-in' in the street

60

oo   Come on   now!   Danc-in' in the street

danc-in' in the street   *div.*   oo oo   oo___   oo___ oo oo

64

danc-in' in the street   *div.*   oo oo   oo___   *ff* danc-in' in the street.   Yeah!

oo   Come on   now!   *ff*

This page may be photocopied

27 I will sing joy!

RESOURCES ▶ CD2 track 4 (performance) and 26 (backing)

Information

Written in an up-tempo gospel style, this song is a guaranteed crowd-pleaser! It is full of devices unique to this idiom, including 'bell-tone pyramids' (bar 13) and a choral breakdown (bars 41–8).

Starting

- Start with some stretches; then do some energy exercises to get the blood flowing and create an upbeat feeling. Try jumping up and down for five seconds and shouting 'way-hay!'. Throw your voices across the room, perhaps following through with an arm movement as if throwing a ball.
- This song is full of long notes that need to be sung through to the end. On the word 'joy', essentially an 'ah' vowel, sing long, single notes. Then try adding more 'aw' to the vowel to make it darker, and 'eh' (as in 'egg') to make it brighter. Settle on a place in between the two.
- Prepare the voice for 'belt' singing with the exercise on p. 55.

Teaching and rehearsing

- Starting at about ♩ = 120, and working up to ♩ = 147, speak then sing the chorus (starting from the pick-up in bar 8a). Make sure the syncopated rhythms are tight and together, and aim for a bright, rounded, rich 'belt' tone with a fast, wide vibrato. Once this is comfortable, add the accompaniment.
- Now do the same with bars 8b–16, which introduces parts. Watch out for the crossed parts in bar 11, and pay close attention to the 'joy' entries in bar 13—work up to the required tempo. Slightly stress the word 'joy' each time. The smaller notes are for basses not comfortable singing the written notes.
- Next, speak and then sing the verses (bars 16 and 40a). The tone here should be warmer and more subdued, with a natural ebb and flow in the dynamics. Ensure that the triplets feel stretched and not rushed. Take care over bars 25–8. Start with the whole group singing the Soprano line; then have the sopranos and baritones sing their parts together. Add the altos and finally some accompaniment.
- Now piece it all together by singing accompanied from the beginning to the end of verse 2 (bar 40b). Note that the first chorus is tacet, with voices coming in on the repeat.
- Speak then sing bars 41–8, starting with the sopranos and adding the other parts one by one. Slightly stress the word 'joy' each time. Start the smears in bars 45–7 softly and grow as you approach the written pitch.
- Take your time teaching bars 54 to the end—the rhythms are challenging but well worth the effort. The rit. in bar 56 should be massive, and beats 2 and 3 should have weight on them. Get back into tempo in bar 58; the fall-off in the last bar should be quick and fade fast.
- Finally, sing the entire piece.

Ideas

- Develop your group's feel for the style by listening to recordings by Richard Smallwood, Israel Houghton, Geron Davis, and other singers of gospel music.

Listen out

- Check that the rhythm is clean and precise.
- In most contemporary gospel music, the men are scored rather high in their range while the women are scored in their chest range. Make sure all parts are balanced and the men don't overpower the women.
- The choruses should be louder than the verses. You want to get your congregation/audience to sing along on the choruses, so each one has more drive and energy than the last. The verses are more intimate, drawing your congregation/audience in to listen; and the breakdown (bars 41–8) is your time to work them into a frenzy!

Performing

- Spacing can make a big difference in performance. Try singing with the group standing close together in a block so that the sound becomes unified and punchy; then try standing a little further apart—perhaps half an arm's length from each other and in two rows. Finally, have everyone stretch their arms out to the sides, so that each person's fingers are just touching the next. Now each singer will sound and feel like a soloist! Allow each member of the group to have a turn listening to the difference, and discuss which sound is best. Which gives the best balance for the audience? And in what positions can you hear each other best?
- Ensure singers are looking, as well as sounding, joyful. This will show in your sound.

27 I will sing joy!

Words: John Moysen and David Major
Music: Steve Milloy

8b
2
S.
A.
I will sing joy, to sing it for peace,
F/C F7 F♯°7 Gm /B♭ F/C
11
I will sing joy
that is my plan. I will sing joy
C♯°7 Dm C9sus F/C F7
joy
14
mf
'n' bring it to each wo - man and man. 1. If we can all
B♭6 /B F/C C9sus F/C C9sus F F9(♯5)/B

Lyrics under the staves:

m. 17–20:
__ sing the same song, then I know we__ can get a-long. And if we all__
__ to the same beat and clap our hands and move our feet, our mel-o-dy mak-

Chords: Bb   F/A

m. 21–24:
__ play the same tune, the day of our dreams__ will come soon. If we could
- in' a big sound, our mes-sage would touch lives_ the world round.

S. only

Chords: Gm   C9sus   F9sus   F7   F9(#5)/B

m. 25–28:

S.
all__ join hands, learn__ the same dance,

A.
If we could all__ join hands, learn__

Bar.
If we could all__ join hands, learn__ the same dance,

Chords: Bb   F/A

29
unis.
f
1
then we'll see, we all will see, we c'd live in har - mo-ny! I will sing joy
Gm F/A B♭ Bm7(♭5) C9sus B♭6/D A♭/E♭ Gm/D F/C F7
f
33a
'n' when I sing joy it will bring joy. I will sing joy
F♯°7 Gm /B♭ F/C C♯°7 Dm C9sus F/C F7
37a
mf
'n' bring it to ev - 'ry girl and boy. 2. If we all sway
B♭6 /B F/C C9sus F/C C9sus F F9(♯5)/B

32b
S.
A.
Bar.
2
- mo - ny! I will sing joy, to sing it for peace,
Ab/Eb Gm/D F/C F7 F#o7 Gm /Bb F/C
35b
I will sing joy
that is my plan. I will sing joy
joy
C#o7 Dm C9sus F/C F7
15ma
38b
'n' bring it to each wo - man and man.
Bb6 /B F/C C9sus F/C C9sus F /C F9

I will sing joy, I will sing joy, I will sing joy!

I will sing joy, I will sing

joy, I will sing joy!

I will sing joy!

I will sing joy!

I will sing joy!

for mak-in' the world

I will sing joy
50
a bet - ter place. I will sing joy, I wan-na bring joy,
joy
C♯°7 Dm C9sus F/C F7
8va
Gm/B♭ /B F/C
rit.
54
bring joy, bring joy 'oy to the whole hu - man
Gm/C F/C Gm/C F/C
rit.
Dm B♭7/A♭ G7 C9sus
58
a tempo
race. Go, sing joy!
a tempo
F B♭7/F
D♭ E♭ E♭maj7 F

27 I will sing joy!

Vocal score

Words: John Moysen and David Major
Music: Steve Milloy

Gospel rock; with joy! ♩ = 147

Chorus
1st time tacet
unis.

(joy)_____ 'n' when I sing joy it__ will bring joy.__ I will sing joy

_____ 'n' bring it to ev - 'ry_ girl and boy I will sing joy_ _ I will sing joy,

(sing)

to sing it for peace, that_ is__ my plan.__ I will sing

I will sing joy_

joy_____ 'n' bring it to each wo - man and_ man.__ 1. If we can all

joy_____

17 *unis.*

_ sing the same song, then I know we_ can get a-long. And if we all_
_ to the same beat and clap our hands and move our feet, our mel-o-dy mak-

21

_ play the same tune, the day of our dreams_ will come soon. *S. only* If we could
- in' a big sound, our mes-sage would touch lives_ the world round.

25

S. all_____ join hands, learn_____ the same dance,

A. If we could all_____ join hands, learn_

Bar. If we could all_____ join hands, learn_____ the same dance,

29 *unis.*

then we'll see, we all_ will see,_ *f* we c'd live in har-mo-ny!_ **1** I will sing joy

33a

_____ 'n' when I sing joy it_ will bring joy._ I will sing joy 'n' bring it to ev - 'ry_ girl_ and_ boy._ 2. If we all sway_

- mo-ny!_ I will sing joy,_____ to sing it for peace, that is_ my plan.

I will sing joy_____

_ I will sing joy_____ 'n' bring it to each wo - man and man._

joy_____

I will sing joy, I will sing joy, I will sing joy! I will sing joy, I will sing

44
joy, I will sing joy!
I will sing joy!
I will sing joy!
I will sing joy!
48
I will sing joy
for mak-in' the world
a bet - ter
place.
I will sing
52
joy,
I wan-na bring joy,
bring joy,
bring joy
joy
rit.
a tempo
56
'oy to the whole
hu-man
race.
Go,
sing joy!

This page may be photocopied
© Oxford University Press 2008

28 It don't mean a thing if it ain't got that swing

RESOURCES ▶ CD2 track 5 (performance) and 27 (backing)

Information

This is a chance for your choir to sing some swing in a 1930s-style arrangement! Duke Ellington's famous standard—one of several signature tunes—was composed in 1932 with his manager Irving Mills. It is also available in famous versions by jazz artists including Ella Fitzgerald, Betty Carter, and even Eva Cassidy! Its use of scat syllables ('do-wup') makes it a fun introduction to vocal improvising, and the spirit and energy of the song works well in a range of concert contexts.

Starting

- Set the scene with one of the short warm ups on swing from Section I.
- Sing some scales of your choice to 'do-ba do-ba do-ba' in a relaxed swing feel, adding weight to the 'ba'.
- Over the intro vamp, sing a single 'do-wup' on beat 2 on F, as in the first time the phrase appears in the tune. Repeat four times on the second beat of the bar. Then move it to the third beat and repeat four times. Try this on all four beats in the bar. Finally, try the pattern in the song, speaking it first and then singing.
- Say the words of the initial phrase to the rhythm, making sure 'a' is really short and the rest after 'thing' is in place.

Teaching and rehearsing

- This song is a 32-bar standard in AABA form. Identify the B bridge (bar 21), then sing each of the A sections with the 'doo-wup' sections in unison to start with, spotting where the melody changes and where it stays the same.
- Work on the 'do-wup' sections part by part, adding each in turn to the Soprano, which stays on the same note. Pitch the starting notes by listening to the 'F' unison on 'swing'. Try singing 'swing' out of time and then immediately sing the 'do-' chord.
- Now work on the bridge. The question and answer between parts is important here. How is the balance? Try to even the parts up as far as possible.
- Speak the rhythm to the 'ba do-bi-doop' section. The 'waa' section (from bar 41) is designed to sound like brass players using plunger mutes. Say 'waa' slowly, enjoying the change in mouth shape and sound. Is the 'aa' a bright sound or a dark sound? Listen to trumpet player Bubber Miley in Ellington recordings from the 1920s and 1930s to get the idea. Explore the different sounds your voice can make using the sound 'waa'.

Ideas

- This is a song about dancing and singing, which should be sung with a 'smile in your voice'. This makes the sound brighter, and it also affects the mood. Spend time telling jokes or laughing, and then try singing while smiling. Hear how the relaxed ease in the room makes the song speak more clearly.
- This was the dance music of the time and would probably have involved some dancing. If you can, get ideas by watching a video of Duke Ellington's band playing the Cotton Club in the 1920s. Perhaps try some simple moves in the piano break. Also research costumes of the time.

Improvising toolbox

- There are optional four-bar spaces over the 'waa's for individuals to try some solo improvising. If you are singing this section more than once (instead of going to the coda at the end of bar 36), consider adding this on the repeat. If singers are unsure where to start, begin by improvising a continuous flow of vocal rhythm (unaccompanied), perhaps using the syllables in the song: 'do', 'wup', 'bup', 'ba', and so on. Experiment with different opening consonants—e.g. 'za' or 'va' instead of 'ba'—then add in some spaces. Finally, add pitch once the flow is confident.

Listen out

- Is the tenor E♮ on 'well' (bar 28) bright enough?
- Listen for dynamics, especially on the sections with hairpins. You can use swing to phrase crisply without necessarily being loud.

Performing

- The arrangement begins with a simple bass-line and builds up, which makes it work well as an opener to bring the group on to. If you have a large group, use the bass-line as an open vamp and simply cue the tune when everyone is in place.

28 It don't mean a thing if it ain't got that swing

Words: Duke Ellington
Music: Irving Mills, arr. Charles Beale

Lyrics: don't mean a thing __ if it ain't got that swing

do wup do wup do wup do wup do wup do wup do wup do wah. It

13
don't mean a thing all you got-ta do is sing
Fm Db7 C7 Fm Fm7
17
unis.
do wup do wup do wup do wup do wup do wup do wup do wah. It
Bb7 Bbm7 D°/Eb Ab Fm7 Em7
21
makes no dif-f'rence if it's sweet or hot bup ba - dup.
T.
B.
bup bup ba - dup. Just
Ebm7 Ab7 Db Ebm7 E° Db/F

37
Ba do-bi-doop boop bah_ ba do-bi-doop boop bah_
mp
oo
Fm
Db7
C7
Fm
opt. solo improvising
41
like muted brass
waa waa waa
mf
f
waa waa waa ba-ber da-ber
Bbm7(b5)
Eb7(b9)
Ab6
C7
45
mf
ba do-bi-doop boop bah_ ba do-bi-doop boop bah_
mp
dap
oo
Fm
Db7
C7
Fm

49
waa waa waa
mf
waa waa waa
Bbm11 Eb7(b9) Ab6 Ab Ab7
f
55
f
bap bah dap ba dap
f
Db6 /C /Cb Bb7 Eb
60
gliss.
bup bow
mf
ba do-bi-doop boop bah
ba do-bi-doop boop bah
gliss.
mp
oo
C7+ Fm Db7 C7 Fm
mf

D.S. al Coda
65
mf
waa
waa
waa
It
mf
waa
waa
waa
D.S. al Coda
Bbm11
Eb7(b9)
Ab6
Ab
Fm7
Em7
CODA
69
pp
do wup do wup do wup do wup do wup do wup do wup do wah
pp
CODA
Bb7
Bbm7
D°/Eb
Ab
F7
pp
73
ff
(whisper)
do wup do wup do wup do wup do wup do wup do wup do wah Yeah!
ff
(whisper)
Bb7
Bbm7
D°/Eb
Ab
8va
ff

28 It don't mean a thing if it ain't got that swing

Vocal score

Words: Duke Ellington
Music: Irving Mills
arr. Charles Beale

Swing. Fast, relaxed ♩ = 200

Opt. open repeat and solo improvising

It don't mean a thing if it ain't got that swing do wup do wup do wup do wup do wup do wup do wup do wah. It don't mean a thing all you got-ta do__ is sing do wup do wup do wup do wup do wup do wup do wup do wah. It makes no dif-f'rence if it's sweet or hot bup ba-dup. bup bup ba-dup. Just give that rhy-thm

This page may be photocopied

Well it don't mean a thing___ if it ev-'ry thing you got.

ain't got that swing do wup do wup do wup do wup do wup

last time **to Coda** ⊕

do wup do wup do wah. Ba do-bi-doop boop bah___

opt. solo improvising

like muted brass

ba do-bi-doop boop bah___ waa waa waa_____

mp   *mf*   *f*

oo_____ waa waa waa_____ ba-ber da-ber

mf

ba do-bi-doop boop bah___ ba do-bi-doop boop bah___

mp

dap oo_____

28. It don't mean a thing if it ain't got that swing

This page may be photocopied

Copyright Acknowledgements

above for purchasers to make photocopies as required, for use by choirs and groups within the purchaser's institution only. All relevant pages are marked 'This page may be photocopied' at the foot. Please note that any page *not* so marked may not be photocopied.

■ CD credits

Vocal tracks

Song nos. 9, 14, and 20
Singers: Steve Milloy, Jennifer Owen, and Kathi Ridley
Keyboard: Steve Milloy
Recorded at Hyde Park Community United Methodist Church, Cincinnati, by Steve Milloy.

Other tracks:
Singers: Charles Beale (No. 5 only), Heather Cairncross, Alexander L'Estrange, Louise Marshall, Steve Milloy, Ben Parry
Piano: Charles Beale; Steve Milloy (Nos. 10 and 13 only). Bass: Alexander L'Estrange.
Drums: Chris Wells
Directed by Charles Beale and Steve Milloy and recorded at the Royal College of Music, London, by Benjamin Wiffens.

Backing tracks

Backing tracks for nos. 7, 9, 14, 16, and 20 were prepared by Steve Milloy; the backing track for no. 22 was prepared by Charles Beale.

All other tracks:
Piano: Charles Beale; Steve Milloy (Nos. 10 and 13 only). Bass: Alexander L'Estrange.
Drums: Chris Wells

Glossary

a cappella: unaccompanied singing

arpeggio: melodic phrase made of the notes of a chord

backbeat: often on beats 2 and 4 in a 4/4 bar and on a bright instrument such as the snare drum, the backbeat creates a question and answer with the bass drum, on beats 1 and 3

backings/backing vocals: a set of vocal parts often consisting in part of words from the song concerned, and in part of 'oo's, 'ah's, and other vocalizations, which back the main melody and add depth to the vocal texture in pop music

blue notes: conventionally the flattened 3rd, 5th, and 7th of a major or minor scale

blues (12–bar): one of the most popular and varied chord progressions in popular music, a popular version (one chord per 4/4 bar) is I, I, I, I, IV, IV, I, I, V, IV, I, I (or V)

bridge: the bit in the middle of a pop song that connects the verse and the chorus

canon (also round): line of music that can be sung against itself, starting at different points within the phrase

changed or changing voices: voices that have developed, or are in the process of developing, a lower pitch range due to changes in physical growth. Sometimes incorrectly called broken voices.

chest voice: the part of the voice that resonates primarily in the chest. It's lower in pitch and usually has a full sound.

chord: group of notes sounding at the same time

chromatic: notes that do not belong to a diatonic scale (such as the major scale of eight notes). A chromatic scale contains all the notes on a keyboard.

consonants: the non-vowel sounds we speak. Some are voiced (with pitch, e.g. 'b' and 'd') and some are un-voiced (unpitched, e.g. 'p' and 't').

counter-melody: melody of secondary importance, which goes against the main melody and interacts with it

counterpoint: the effect of two or more independent vocal lines working together to form a whole

crescendo: Italian term meaning 'growing', used to indicate a gradual increase in sound level

decrescendo/diminuendo: Italian terms used to indicate getting gradually quieter

diaphragm: dome-shaped sheet of muscle that sits below the rib-cage and pulls up and down to create air pressure, supporting the vocal sound

diatonic: notes of the scale that belong in the key (not chromatic notes)

Dorian mode: slightly minor-sounding mode that has semitones between the 2nd and 3rd, and 6th and 7th, degrees of the scale. May be built from the 2nd degree of the major scale, e.g. D Dorian contains the pitches of C major.

downbeat/upbeat: usually the first beat of the bar. The upbeat is often the beat before the downbeat and is felt as leading to it.

doo-wop: style of rhythm and blues music that originated from African Americans and was popular from the mid-1950s to the early 1960s. The term refers to the ad-lib syllables used in the backing harmonies.

dynamics: indication of different levels of sound or volume

fall-off: descending sigh usually followed by a rest. It should have a relaxed quality and end softer than it began.

falsetto: a singing technique usually used by men, whereby a lighter, softer, and often more high-pitched sound is created by using different parts of the vocal cords.

float: to sing with a light, heady quality

foldback: the amplification of sound, often voices, via a second set of speakers pointing back at the performers, which allows them to hear the amplified sound as they sing live into microphones; helps balance and tuning especially

glissando: sliding up or down in pitch (*see also* 'smear' and 'fall-off')

groove: a repeating set of rhythmic patterns played around a pulse by a rhythm section, the groove defines the musical character of a song and drives it forward. Common grooves include swing, rock, funk, and samba.

head voice: a phrase many singing teachers use to refer to the part of the voice that resonates primarily in the head. It's the highest part of the natural range.

improvising: a musical activity where musical elements such as rhythm and pitch are chosen in the moment to create a spontaneous piece of music, often over a chord sequence or groove

interval: the distance between two notes

intro: short for introduction, the opening lead into a song (*see also* 'outro')

inversion: placing the notes of a chord in a different order

legato: smoothly

melisma: singing one syllable to a series of notes

middle 8: the middle section of a pop song, often but not always eight bars long and sometimes an instrumental solo. It provides contrast from the melodies and often comes after verse, bridge, and repeated choruses.

modulation: moving from one key to another

monotone: one note (singing a melody to one note)

motive: a short melodic idea, which forms the basis for a longer musical structure through, e.g. being repeated, developed, or modified

obligato: an extra and sometimes optional line, often above the melody; an example of a counter-melody

ostinato: short, repetitive rhythmic pattern

outro: the part at the end of a performance of a pop song—sometimes repeated choruses, and sometimes a coda which may or may not mirror the intro

part-leading: the music line created by each individual voice

part-singing: different vocal lines sung at the same time

pentatonic: based on the pentatonic scale—a scale consisting of five notes (e.g. CDEFG)

phrasing: singing in phrases—i.e. lines of music sung in one breath; notes that should be connected together to make musical sense (like a spoken sentence, punctuated by commas and full-stops)

pitch: the sound of notes relative to each other, high or low. Technically, it is determined by the vibrations per second of the sound.

register: an area of the voice where the vocal quality is the same; a group of adjacent notes sung with the same tonal quality

resonance: the sound created by a voice when, through using parts of the head or whole body as an amplifier, the vocal sound is made richer and more full of character

riff: single simple repeating melodic pattern, often used in combination to create a contrapuntal rhythmic texture

root position: the tonic note of a chord sounding in the lowest voice

rote: learning of music (by ear) by repetition until secure

round: *see* 'canon'

scat: the process of vocal improvising using made-up words and syllables to add rhythmic character

slide/smear: vocal inflection in which you start a pitch lower than written (usually a whole step or lower) and slide to the written pitch within the length of the written note

soft palate: tissue at the back of the roof of the mouth

speech-level singing: approach to singing in which the larynx (voice box) is kept in the same position as in speaking

staccato: Italian term meaning 'detached'; notes should be shortened with gaps between them

subdivision: the process by which a beat is divided up, e.g. into two parts (quavers/eighth notes), three parts (triplets), or four parts (semiquavers/sixteenth notes)

support: the air pressure that forms the basis of a steady sound

swing; swing quavers/eighth notes: a subdivision, often of a 4/4 bar, where the offbeat quaver occurs as a relaxed triplet and is sometimes given added weight. Mostly legato.

syncopation: using or accenting offbeats, often asymmetrically, to produce catchy and exciting rhythms

tag: concluding section to a song, where a small part is repeated and sometimes developed (often three times, as in No. 6 'Deed I Do)

texture: the quality of the overall sound—its 'thickness' or 'thinness'. This can be produced e.g. by different combinations of voices singing together, the amount of movement in each part, and the type of harmony and the pitch of the parts.

tonic: the first or root note of a key; the 'home' note to which the other notes in that key are related. The key a piece starts in, and often ends in too.

triad: chord made up of three notes

unison: when all parts sing the same tune together. Rhythmic unison is when the parts have the same rhythm but not necessarily the same notes.

upbeat: *see* 'downbeat'

vibrato: a pulsating change in pitch and/or volume, said by many to be natural to the singing voice. The width and exact position of vibrato on a note varies from style to style.

voice leading: the route any one voice part follows through the music, creating cadential feelings of tension and release. For example, the 'leading note', or 7th degree, feels tense and should rise to the tonic, where it feels resolved.

vowel: the open sounds in words, such as A, E, I, O, and U and other secondary vowels, on which longer pitches are often placed

whole tone: the step from one note to another equivalent to two semitones (e.g. C to D). A whole-tone scale consists only of steps of a tone, giving six notes an octave.